Presented To

_____

On

_____

By

_____

LIFE ON PURPOSE™ DEVOTIONAL FOR WOMEN

*Practical Faith and Profound Insight
for Every Day*

By
J.M. Farro

Harrison House
Tulsa, OK

06 05 04   10 9 8 7 6 5 4 3 2 1

Life on Purpose™ Devotional for Women:
Practical Faith and Profound Insight for Every Day
ISBN 1-57794-649-9
Copyright © 2004 by J.M. Farro
P.O. Box 434
Nazareth, PA 18064

Published by **Harrison House, Inc.**
P.O. Box 35035
Tulsa, OK 74153

Contents

New Beginnings 1

Shut Up and Pray 4

Winning Battles God's Way 7

Following God's Peace 9

An Example of the Abundant Life....................................12

Let Go and Let God 15

God's Winning Strategy...18

Learning To Be Content 21

One Step at a Time 24

Believe and See His Glory 27

Needs Vs. Wants 29

The Difference That Trust Makes 31

Making Way for the New 34

Praying God's Will 37

Overlooked and Unappreciated 40

Our Giving God 43

God Cares About the Details..46

Dating: One Mom's Perspective 49

Pour on the Love 52

Do You Want To Get Well? 55

Nothing Can Hinder the Lord 58

Faith for Major Decisions 61

Turning the Tables on the Enemy 64

The Difference Humility Can Make...................................67

Blessed To Impress..70

Prayer That Gets Results 73

Extra Goodies..75

The Dangers of Strife..77

Getting Alone With God 80

Testing Will Surely Come 84

The Proper Faith Response 86

Stubbornness Vs. Surrender 89

Waiting for God's Best..92

Faithful in Little Things..94

Our Rightful Source..97

The High Cost of Unforgiveness 99

The Positive Power of Saying "No" 101

You Can't Please People...104

Faith Doesn't Need the "Big Picture" 107

You Have a Job To Do! 109

When Trouble Strikes 111

The Price of Peace Is Prayer 114

You Will Know Them by Their Fruit 116

The Recipe for Success..119

Wait for the Harvest 121

When All We Can See Are Giants! 124

The God of Comfort...126

The Lord Will Provide 129

Spirit-Led Prayer 132

Keeping Our Dreams in Proper Perspective 135

Breaking Destructive Patterns 138

When Words Are Many 141

Good Reason To Hope 144

The Lord Can Give You Much More 147

The Power of Joy 150

Hearing the Good Shepherd's Voice 153

Cast Those Cares 156

Faith Is Spelled "R-I-S-K" 159

By the Obedience of One...162

Who Needs Signs? 165

A Message of Restoration 167

Rejoicing in Our Labor 169

Equipped for Service 172

God's Healing Word...175

Anger Vs. Assistance 178

Let Your Light Shine 181

Not Perfect? Read This! 184

Strength in Adversity..187

According to Your Faith...190

Grace Under Pressure 193

The High Cost of Complaining 196

Prophesying Our Future 199

In Times of Betrayal and Injustice 202

From Trials to Triumphs 204

"Ungodly" Invitations 206

A Prophet Without Honor 208

Fulfilling Our God-Given Purpose..210

He Lifts Us Up..213

Dependence Vs. Independence 215

Saying "No" to Self-Pity..218

An Invitation to Criticism 221

Don't Get Offended 223

The Power of God's Word 225

Even Now..228

Don't Get Lazy...230

New Beginnings

{ *Forget the former things; do not dwell on the past. See, I am doing a new thing! Now it springs up; do you not perceive it.* }

ISAIAH 43:18,19

Two years ago my older son, Joseph, moved out of our home. Coping with his absence alone would have been difficult enough, but around the same time of his departure, my younger son, John, graduated from high school. John was going to remain at home and attend a local college, and I was grateful for that. But his high school graduation would mark the end of my family's involvement with the Bible club my older son started five years earlier. During those years my life had been filled with countless club-related tasks, including driving teens home from weekly meetings, helping my sons put together Bible lessons, holding parties in my home for the kids, and organizing frequent concert trips. Once it was all over my life began to seem empty, purposeless, and meaningless. Feelings of being unneeded and unwanted overwhelmed me, and I didn't know how to stop the downward spiral I found myself in.

During this time I cried out to the Lord in desperation and despair. It was then that He showed me the above verses in Isaiah 43. He revealed to me that He wanted to do a "new thing" in my life, but first I had to "forget the former things" and "not dwell on the past." God's awesome new plans for me would not unfold until I stopped feeling sorry for myself and let go of all the negative emotions associated with my profound sense of loss. I had to determine to put the past behind me and believe that God had wonderful plans ahead for me, or I would never "perceive" the "new thing" He wanted to do in my life. It wasn't easy for me. I kept thinking about all the special times I had shared with my son over the past 20 years, as well as all the wonderful experiences I had had through my involvement with the Bible club. There were times I doubted that I would ever recover from my sense of loss. But as I prayed and depended upon God's grace to heal me and to help me let go of the past, the Lord began to unfold the "new thing" He had planned for me. Today my life is filled with more purpose and meaning than I ever dreamed possible, and I shudder to think of all the blessings I would have missed out on if I hadn't cooperated with God for my deliverance. If you are feeling today that your life is empty, meaningless, or purposeless because of your past experiences or a sense of loss, please know that God has awesome plans for your life. He says, "For I know the plans I have for you—plans to prosper you and not to harm you, plans to give you hope and a future" (Jer. 29:11). It doesn't matter how old you are or what your background is—God is able to fill your life with new purpose and meaning. Start asking Him to do something new and wonderful in your life. Trust Him to begin revealing the "new thing" He has planned for you as you determine to let go of what lies behind and reach out for what lies ahead. Remember

LIVE ON PURPOSE TODAY

Take some time today to reflect on your dreams, and write down your top three goals. Keep them in a place where you can refer to them often—in your Bible or nightstand perhaps. Pray about them, and begin to take steps toward them as the Lord leads you.

that endings pave the way for new beginnings. Today, be encouraged by this precious promise from God: "Arise [from the depression and prostration in which circumstances have kept you—rise to a new life]! Shine (be radiant with the glory of the Lord), for your light has come, and the glory of the Lord has risen upon you!" (Isa. 60:1 AMP).

PRAYER

Lord, I ask that You give me a new awareness of the awesome plans You have for my life. Help me to stop dwelling on the past, and to let go of all regret, sorrow, and bitterness. Fill my life with new purpose and meaning, and use me to make a difference in people's lives for Your glory. Thank You for a new beginning and a fresh start!

Fun+Play- YEAR 20--?
purpose
be a light in their darkness

3/2/23
I DON't even remember starting this book—a some time long ago

Started today to refocus my Brain + find purpose

Love this - going to try it instead of putting a specific thorn under the rug

Shut Up and Pray

This is the confidence we have in approaching God: that if we ask anything according to his will, he hears us. And if we know that he hears us—whatever we ask— we know that we have what we asked of him.

1 JOHN 5:14,15

Some years ago my husband, Joe, and his sister had a serious disagreement, and as a result, they stopped speaking to each other. I tried several times to intervene and bring them back together, but every attempt of mine failed. Whenever I tried talking to my husband about reconciling with his sister, I was met with increasing resistance. I finally put the matter in the Lord's hands and told Him that I was counting on His help. I began to earnestly pray for reconciliation, but I didn't talk to my husband about it. One morning Joe confessed to me that he had a dream about making peace with his sister. He began sharing with me how often he thought of her and how he felt like the Lord might be leading him to call her. Finally, the day came when he did just that. His sister wasn't as receptive as he had hoped, but with the Lord's help, Joe lovingly persisted and they have enjoyed a peaceful relationship ever since.

For the past ten years my husband has worked part-time for a large tax preparation firm during tax season. He's done this in addition to his full-time job. Every year during tax season our kids and I knew we weren't going to see much of their dad. Besides that, Joe had to work on Sundays, which made it very difficult for us to attend church as a family. I often complained about his second job and pleaded with him to quit. But no matter what I said or did, he refused. This year I decided to put the matter in God's hands, and I began praying earnestly that He would make a way for my husband to leave his part-time job. After several weeks, when Joe began complaining about all the negative changes that were being made in his company, I casually suggested that perhaps it was God's will for him to finally quit. I was stunned when my husband went into work the following day and gave his notice. I had read about the "shut up and pray" principle, and I believed it was the strategy God wanted me to employ in both of these situations. I was relatively certain that I was praying according to God's will, and I claimed God's promise in the verses above. But to be honest, I wasn't completely sure until I witnessed the Lord's supernatural intervention. David prayed, "Set a guard over my mouth, O Lord; keep watch over the door of my lips" (Ps. 141:3). If we pressure people or say the wrong things when we want them to change their behavior or course of action, we can make them more stubborn and resistant.

LIVE ON PURPOSE TODAY

Check your heart and see if there is anyone you've been trying to change. If there is, take a moment right now to pray for him or her. Paul's prayer in Ephesians 1:17-23 is a perfect prayer for those who need change in their life.

In these cases, we're not helping God; we're hindering Him. Often the Lord won't get involved in matters like these until we back off and hand them completely over to Him. If we stop trying to accomplish what only God can, and if we invite Him into the situation through fervent prayer, He will do what we can't. He knows how to reach these people even when we don't, and He can put pressure on them in ways that will turn their hearts toward—not against—Him and us. If we're ever tempted to harbor bitterness or resentment against the people involved, we must repent and ask for God's forgiveness and help; otherwise our prayers won't be very effective. If you feel like you've tried everything to get someone to change their behavior or course of action and you've gotten nowhere, let me encourage you to entrust the matter to the Lord, "enter His rest," and "cease from your own labors" (Heb. 4:3,10). Persevere in prayer, then be prepared to witness the miracle-working power of God!

PRAYER

Lord, show me when to confront someone about their behavior, and when to just be silent and pray for them. Help me to do my part and to let You do Yours. When I'm tempted to hold anything against anyone, help me to forgive them quickly and thoroughly. Thank You that because of my right-standing with You in Christ Jesus, my prayers shall have "great power and wonderful results"! (James 5:16 TLB).

Winning Battles God's Way

Do not say, "I'll pay you back for this wrong!"
Wait for the Lord, and he will deliver you.

PROVERBS 20:22

It seems that one of the hardest things for us to do is to wait for God to deliver us when we are victims of wrongdoing. Often our first reaction is to become angry, offended, or to retaliate somehow. Unfortunately, when we do that, we usually forfeit any help we might have gotten from the Lord. God taught me something about this through a painful lesson a few years ago. My husband and I moved to a new home, and our two young sons began to get acquainted with the other kids in the neighborhood. At first we were delighted that our children were making new friends, but it wasn't too long before we realized that the neighborhood kids were often mischievous, and even malicious at times. We finally told our sons that they were no longer allowed to associate with the neighborhood gang. My husband and I were as gracious about this as possible, but our neighbors became offended and their children began threatening our kids and attacking our home and property, doing serious damage. When trying to reason with them didn't work, we resorted to calling on the police for help. Not only did that fail to work, but it actually made the problem—and the attacks—worse. All this time I prayed and stood on God's promises for deliverance, while my husband became more and more bitter and contemplated taking matters into his own hands. Then one night we caught one of the troublesome kids red-handed, and we filed charges against him. His parents

LIVE ON PURPOSE TODAY

Are you a victim of injustice? If so, make a concrete decision this very moment to follow God's lead in the matter. Father always knows best!

came to my husband late that night, pleading with him to drop the charges against their son. I was amazed when my husband agreed and sent that family home, relieved and grateful. The police were not pleased with my husband's decision. They warned us that we had given up our only chance to stop the attacks on our home and family. But since that night we have lived here in peace. In addition, the Lord restored our home by causing our insurance company to put all new siding on our house. Since then, whenever my family and I encounter injustice of any kind, we seek God's direction and depend on Him to vindicate us. Yes, there are times we may have to take appropriate action—perhaps even legal action—but it should only be at God's direction and with His approval. Otherwise, it will be futile, or even disastrous. If you are in need of deliverance from injustice today, be encouraged by God's promise to you: "The Lord will vindicate his people and have compassion on his servants" (Ps. 135:14).

PRAYER

Lord, when I'm a victim of injustice, help me to seek Your direction above everyone else's. Show me when to take appropriate action and when to wait on You for deliverance. Teach me how to let You fight my battles for me so that I can gain the victory every time. Thank You for promising to be my Vindicator!

Following God's Peace

Let the peace (soul harmony which comes) from Christ rule
(act as umpire continually) in your hearts, deciding
with finality all questions that arise in your minds....

COLOSSIANS 3:15 AMP

Last summer I began experiencing some health problems that made it necessary for me to limit some of my activities, even with my doctor's care and prayer. My husband, Joe, and I already had a vacation planned with our oldest son and his wife. This trip involved a lengthy car ride, as well as a couple of nights in a hotel far from home. Even though I had misgivings about this trip, I pushed them aside as I thought about how disappointed my family would be if I told them I couldn't go. I prayed that the Lord would enable me to make this trip without any problems, and I asked my loved ones and fellow prayer warriors to keep me covered in prayer. Even so, within the first few hours of our departure, I got very sick, and I spent the rest of the day and night in bed in my hotel room. The next morning, as soon as I was able to travel, we headed back home, sorely disappointed that our trip had to be cut short.

After a lot of prayer and soul-searching, I realized that the Lord had given me plenty of warnings in advance that I should have canceled that trip, no matter how it might have disappointed my loved ones. Taking that trip was not a wise thing to do, and all the faith and prayer in the world were not going to change that. It was a painful but very valuable lesson for me. It made me realize that stepping out in faith is a wonderful thing—and something that God often asks and expects us to do. But it's also wonderful in His sight when we use godly wisdom, and when we recognize that we don't have peace about doing something we have prayed and sought God about. The Bible says, "Let the peace of God rule in your hearts" (Col. 3:15 NKJV). The Amplified translation puts it this way: "Let the peace (soul harmony which comes) from Christ rule (act as umpire continually) in your hearts, deciding with finality all questions that arise in your minds…." In my heart, I *knew* that going on that trip was not a good idea, but I did it anyway and suffered the consequences. (And so did my loved ones.) The fact is, when we don't have peace in our hearts about doing something, there's usually a good reason for it. It's true that the Lord will often ask us to step out in faith and do something that makes us fearful and anxious. But even during those times we should have an inner peace that says, "Yes, this feels right. I do believe this is what God wants me to do." And the Lord's presence and power will be there to enable and sustain us. I've seen well-meaning Christians make horrendous mistakes they could have avoided if they had just used some godly wisdom. Somehow they've gotten the notion that whenever God asks them to step out in faith, He's always going to lead them to do something that is irrational or unreasonable. They seem to have forgotten that the Bible says, "Wisdom is supreme; therefore, get wisdom. Though it

LIVE ON PURPOSE TODAY

It's time to ask yourself a straightforward question: Is your heart pricking you in some way? Are you brushing aside any misgivings? Get quiet today, and listen to your heart talk!

cost all you have, get understanding" (Prov. 4:7). The Living Bible puts it this way: "Getting wisdom is the most important thing you can do! And with your wisdom, develop common sense and good judgment" (Prov. 4:7 TLB). When we act in faith, God doesn't expect us to bypass our intellect. He still expects us to seek Him for godly wisdom and discernment in everything we do. That's why Scripture says, "If you want to know what God wants you to do, ask Him, and He will gladly tell you, for He is always ready to give a bountiful supply of wisdom to all who ask Him; He will not resent it" (James 1:5 TLB). The next time you're faced with a decision to make, I hope you'll rely on God's peace—as well as His wisdom—to guide you. For it's in the paths of peace that you'll find His very best blessings!

PRAYER

Lord, whenever I need to make a decision, remind me to turn to You for godly wisdom and guidance. When I sense an absence of peace about a certain course of action, remind me to pause and wait for further instructions from You. Thank You, Lord, that as I follow Your peace, Your blessings will follow me!

An Example of the Abundant Life

*"I came that they may have and enjoy life, and
have it in abundance (to the full, till it overflows)."*

JOHN 10:10 AMP

I have a dear friend, Peggy, who is showered with blessings
wherever she goes. I have never known anyone who was living
the "abundant life" quite like this dear lady is. She is a true
inspiration to me and to countless other believers, and I admire
her immensely. We were chatting together the other day, and we
began discussing what it could be that enabled Peggy to be blessed
"exceedingly abundantly above all that we ask or think" (Eph.
3:20 KJV). We decided that one possible reason was the fact that
Peggy always *expects* to be blessed. I've often heard her say, "God
loves an expectant heart," and I believe this is true. She says that
she always holds her "umbrella" upside down to catch showers of
blessings from heaven. She has no problem receiving from the
Lord, as some of us do, so she is always ready and willing to
accept the good things He offers.

Peggy prays BIG prayers. She sees her God as a BIG God—an
all-powerful God, with whom nothing is impossible. (Luke 1:37
KJV.) She doesn't put limits or restrictions on God. She gives Him
plenty of room to work in every matter she prays about. And she
always has a positive outlook, no matter how hopeless a situation
seems. She truly believes that no matter how bleak the circumstances appear, God will turn them into good for her and other

believers. (Rom. 8:28 KJV.) Another reason that Peggy is so blessed may be because she believes God *desires* to bless her, simply because she has a personal relationship with Him, and not because she does everything right. Peggy is not perfect. But she is the perfect example of someone who is truly "abiding" in Christ and living in union with Him every moment of every day. (John 15:5 KJV.) Peggy prays about everything. (Phil. 4:6 KJV.) She doesn't view any matter as too small or insignificant to bring to the Lord in prayer, and she does her best to be sensitive and obedient to His leading at all times. When she does sin, she is quick to repent and receive God's forgiveness. (1 John 1:9 KJV.) She doesn't dwell on her mistakes, and it is very rare when she allows herself to be over-whelmed by guilt and condemnation. Peggy's relationship with the Lord is the most important thing in her life, and she is committed to doing whatever she needs to in order to maintain a vibrant and intimate relationship with Him. Perhaps most impor-tantly, Peggy is always quick to give God the thanks and the praise for all of her blessings. (Eph. 5:20 KJV.) She feels that more believers would be blessed if they would acknowledge to the Lord—and others—that every good thing that comes their way is from Him. (James 1:17 KJV.) Even if a blessing that she didn't pray for or expect comes her way, she

LIVE ON PURPOSE TODAY

Can you think of someone with whom you've only exchanged pleasantries, yet you've thought, *Hmm, I see God in her, and I seem drawn. I'd like to get to know her better.* Then don't delay! Consider inviting her for coffee or lunch—knowing that God arranges divine connections in your behalf.

promptly and sincerely thanks God for it. She never uses rationale or reasoning to "explain away" the good things she receives daily. She always maintains "an attitude of gratitude," and the Lord continually honors and rewards her for it. When someone comments on Peggy's extraordinarily blessed life in her presence, she always tells them, "God is no respecter of persons. What He does for me, He'll do for you!" Peggy doesn't just say that to try to make people feel better—she knows that God says it in His Word, so it must be true. (Acts 10:34 KJV.) She has a sincere love for the Scriptures, and she takes every promise from God personally. If you don't have someone in your life like Peggy to encourage and inspire you, I hope you'll pray and ask the Lord to send you someone. Better yet, ask God to help *you* be a shining example of someone who is living the abundant life in Christ!

PRAYER

Lord Jesus, You said that You came so that I could live the abundant life, and I ask You to teach me how to do exactly that. Surround me with people who will challenge and inspire me to live a blessed life that will draw others to You. Expand my vision, and enable me to see You as the big, loving, and giving God You are. Thank You, Lord, that what You've done for Peggy, You will do for me!

Let Go and Let God

*While God was testing him, Abraham still trusted in
God and His promises, and so he offered up his son....*

HEBREWS 11:17 TLB

A few years ago I was at the lowest point in my life as a
parent. My older son, Joseph, was at a very rebellious
stage, and no matter how I prayed or sought the Lord,
nothing seemed to help. As I tuned in to one of my favorite TV
ministry programs, I heard the preacher speak Holy Spirit-inspired
words about my situation that would change my life and my
family forever. I'd like to share those words with you today: "Some
of you have kids who are old enough to be hearing from God, and
it's time that you offered those children up to the Lord as a sacrifice, and released them into His care. Even if your kids are off
track now, let go of them, and let God do something—as you put
your trust in Him—to make those children do what's right." I felt
so sure that the Lord was speaking these words to me personally
that I copied them down and asked Him to give me confirmation.
That's when God showed me Hebrews 11:17 TLB: "While God was
testing him, Abraham still trusted in God and His promises, and
so he offered up his son...." For the past six years I had been
praying and standing on God's promises for Joseph. Now it was
time for me to offer him up to the Lord as a sacrifice so that He
could do in my son's life what He needed to. As fearful as I was, I
put Joseph completely in God's hands. Exactly one month later my
husband asked our son to leave our home. Even though I felt like
my heart was breaking, I knew that this was God's will for us as a

family, and I supported my husband's decision. It was time to "let go and let God."

Job 36:15 NLT says, "By means of their suffering, [God] rescues those who suffer. For he gets their attention through adversity." When my son left home, I experienced a period of intense suffering, and during this time God had my undivided attention. As painful as this time was for me, I trusted the Lord to bring good out of it for me and my family. As I sought Him daily through prayer and Bible reading, God showed me that my son had become a kind of idol to me. When He led me to Jesus' words in Matthew 10:37, I felt convicted. "Anyone who loves his son or daughter more than Me is not worthy of Me." Until that moment I hadn't realized that I had often demonstrated more love and devotion for my son than for God. And God was not about to play second fiddle in the life of one who had professed Christ as their Lord and Savior. I immediately confessed my sin and committed myself to put God first from that moment on, with His help. It was then that God gave me a promise to stand on for the restoration of my

LIVE ON PURPOSE TODAY

Check your heart today and make sure that no one holds a larger portion than God Himself. It's best that way— best for you and your family.

family. "The Lord spoke to me again, saying: In Ramah there is bitter weeping—Rachel weeping for her children and cannot be comforted, for they are gone. But the Lord says: Don't cry any longer, for I have heard your prayers and you will see them again; they will come back to you from the distant land of the enemy. There is hope for your future, says the Lord, and your children will come again to their own land" (Jer. 31:15-17 TLB). This promise from God, along with many others, gave me the encouragement and hope I needed to stand in faith for the healing of my family. Though we've endured some periods of estrangement, tension, and conflict, God has worked wonders in restoring our family. And we continue to seek and trust the Lord to help us please and glorify Him more and more. Last month Joseph married Miriam, a godly young woman who brings out the best in my son and is truly an answer to prayer. I hope and pray this message will encourage you to let go of the loved ones in your life that the Lord is asking you to, so that He may perform the work and wonders that will ultimately bless you and glorify Him.

PRAYER

Lord, reveal to me today how this message applies to my life. Give me the strength and courage I need to let go of the loved ones You want me to. Remind me that as long as I'm holding on to them too tightly, You can't do the good work in them or me that You long to do. Thank You that as I choose to "let go and let God," we will be blessed and You will be glorified!

God's Winning Strategy

For the Lord is a God of justice. Blessed are all who wait for him!

ISAIAH 30:18

Recently, the vacuum cleaner I use most around my house died suddenly. I had bought it only three months before, so I was hopeful that the manufacturer would repair it for me at no cost. But when I arrived at the service center with my vacuum and sales receipt, I was told that no claim could be filed without a proper warranty. In front of the service clerk, I flipped through the paperwork that came with my vacuum. To my dismay, I discovered that I had neglected to fill out and mail in the original warranty form. The clerk somberly informed me that she would contact the manufacturer, but that I shouldn't be too hopeful. In the meantime, I prayed and asked the Lord to intervene and make a way for my vacuum to be restored. I also asked Him to forgive me for neglecting to register my warranty. Three days later I still hadn't heard from the service center, so I called and asked what the status of my complaint was. The clerk informed me that my vacuum was beyond repair, and they still hadn't gotten permission from the manufacturer to proceed with my appeal. As soon as I hung up the phone I went to the Lord in prayer, earnestly praying for Him to bring a swift and favorable conclusion to this matter. I reminded Him of His promises of victory and justice, and I told Him that I was counting on His help. Only a few minutes after I finished my prayer I received a call from the service center inform-ing me that the manufacturer had decided to give me a brand-new vacuum for free. I picked up my new machine that very afternoon, and I rejoiced and praised God for His awesome power and mercy.

I believe that in situations like these, God has specific strategies that He wants us to employ. One of them is to refuse to become angry or offended. Proverbs 19:11 TLB says, "A wise man restrains his anger and overlooks insults." And Proverbs 19:19 TLB says, "A short-tempered man must bear his own penalty." When I first approached the service clerk with my complaint, she was uncooperative and even insulting. I was sorely tempted to become indignant, but instead I responded calmly and respectfully, and I believe it made all the difference in the outcome. In Matthew 10:16, Jesus told His disciples, "I am sending you out like sheep among wolves. Therefore be as shrewd as snakes and as innocent as doves." Because there will be times when we have to deal with people who would take advantage of us or deceive us, God wants us to be on our guard and to use wisdom. But that's not an excuse for us to use trickery or deception to try to get our way. We can claim God's promise in Luke 21:15, where Jesus says, "I will give you words and wisdom that none of your adversaries will be able to resist or contradict." The Lord knows exactly what it will take to bring about a favorable outcome in our situation, and He'll show us what to say and do when we seek His help. I once heard someone say that Christians lose more battles because they don't

LIVE ON PURPOSE TODAY

Stop! **This very moment it's time to hand over to the Lord the battles you've tried to fight that you should allow Him to win. Pray right now, and roll the whole of your care upon Him.**

let God do their fighting for them. I believe that's true. There are many verses in the Bible that indicate that God is willing and able to do battle for us. One of my favorites is Exodus 14:14 AMP: "The Lord will fight for you, and you shall hold your peace and remain at rest." Whether our battles are big or small, we should commit them to the Lord and ask Him to fight for us and show us what our part might be. It's important in times like these that we resist becoming fearful or anxious, because fear can cause us to react rashly, and to make poor decisions and costly mistakes. Fear can also make it more difficult for us to receive direction from the Lord. It's wiser for us to pray and stand on God's promises of victory, including Deuteronomy 28:13, which says, "You shall always have the upper hand." Most of all, we should remember that we are never to count on others to execute justice for us apart from God. For as Proverbs 29:26 says, "Many seek an audience with a ruler, but it is from the Lord that man gets justice."

PRAYER

Lord, whenever I'm tempted to fight my own battles, remind me that You are more than willing and able to help me. Show me what my part is in the process, and keep me from becoming angry, offended, or fearful. Thank You that as I employ your strategies and put my trust in You, You'll reveal Yourself to me as Jehovah-Nissi— "The Lord my Victory and my Banner"! (Ex. 17:15).

Learning To Be Content

I know what it is to be in need, and I know what it is to have plenty. I have learned the secret of being content in any and every situation, whether well fed or hungry, whether living in plenty or in want. I can do everything through Him who gives me strength.

PHILIPPIANS 4:12,13

A dear neighbor of mine recently went through a long period of debilitating health problems. During this time she resigned from her executive position with a large company, because she felt that her stressful working conditions were contributing to her declining health. Though this period of joblessness was very difficult for her, she took comfort in the fact that her health was steadily improving. She told me how she had learned to appreciate her health more, and how her trials had helped her to focus less on her career and finances, and more on the things in life that were really important. When a prestigious company sought to hire her but offered her less money than she felt she deserved, she began to think about her many years of schooling and her work-related achievements, and suddenly her career and finances became her main focus once again. I tried to remind her of the new perspective she had gained as a result of her long illness, but she was unreceptive. A few days later a routine medical exam revealed that she had a high risk of developing a life-threatening disease in the future. Once again, she experienced a major change in her values and priorities.

When we read the Bible accounts of the children of Israel, and how they never seemed to be satisfied with the blessings of God, it's easy for us to think, *Nobody could please these people!* But how often are we guilty of the same attitudes? The Bible has a lot to say about contentment. One reason for this is that being content is a good way to avoid loving money or being greedy. Solomon wrote, "Whoever loves money never has money enough; whoever loves wealth is never satisfied with his income. This too is meaningless" (Eccl. 5:10). John the Baptist said simply, "Be content with your pay" (Luke 3:14). This doesn't mean that we should never want to make progress or to increase. It means that we should be led by God's Spirit in these matters and not driven by our fleshly desires. The apostle Paul often spoke about the importance of being content. He wrote, "But godliness with contentment is great gain.... People who want to get rich fall into temptation and a trap, and into many foolish and harmful desires that plunge men into ruin and destruction. For the love of money is a root of all kinds of evil. Some people have wandered from the faith and pierced themselves with many griefs" (1 Tim. 6:6-10). Giving money too much importance will lead us away from God and into sin. The Lord wants to be our Provider, and He wants us to look to Him for all our needs. He takes it personally when we are so dissatisfied with our situation that we neglect to count our blessings. Paul said, "I have learned to be

LIVE ON PURPOSE TODAY

Often the best way to become content with what you do have, is to recognize how much others do not have. Allow the Lord to bring someone in need across your heart today, and then ask Him to direct you with the supply.

content whatever the circumstances" (Phil. 4:11). He also wrote, "I have learned the secret of being content in any and every situation" (Phil. 4:12). Notice that Paul used the word "learned." God had to teach him how to be content at all times, and He will teach us too, if we'll let Him. Paul's "secret" to contentment is revealed in the following verse: "I can do all things through Christ who strengthens me" (Phil. 4:13 NKJV). As we lean on the Lord and cooperate with His plan to make us more like Christ, He will give us the grace we need to maintain an inner peace and contentment in every situation we face. May this promise from God encourage you today: "Keep your lives free from the love of money and be content with what you have, because God has said, 'Never will I leave you; never will I forsake you'"! (Heb. 13:5).

PRAYER

Lord, forgive me for the times I've refused to be content with the blessings You so richly and regularly bestow on me. Give me a godly desire to progress and prosper, but help me to wait for Your will and timing. Teach me to look to You for all my needs, and guard me from a love of money. Thank You for teaching me the secret of being content in every situation!

One Step at a Time

*Be strong and courageous, and do the work. Don't be afraid
or discouraged by the size of the task, for the Lord God,
my God, is with you. He will not fail you or forsake you.
He will see to it that all the work...is finished correctly.*

1 CHRONICLES 28:20 NLT

Once when I was at a wedding with family members years
ago, I was speaking to my Aunt Peggy about my fears,
worries, and concerns. She took my hand and led me to a
long staircase in the restaurant in which we were dining. As we
stood at the bottom, that flight of stairs loomed before us and
looked endless. She pointed to them and told me not to look at the
top or the middle, but only at the first step or two. She said that if
I tried to take all the steps at once, I would fall. But if I took just
one step at a time, I would eventually make it to the top. I often
think of that lesson from my Aunt Peggy when I'm faced with difficult or scary tasks, and it helps me to put things in perspective.

The Lord reminded me of this lesson from my aunt recently
when I had allowed my household chores to pile up to an alarm-
ing degree. Each time I thought about tackling the mountain of
tasks that had accumulated, feelings of fear and dread would overwhelm me. After seeking the Lord in prayer, He instructed me to
start out small by concentrating on only one room at a time,
instead of the entire house all at once. Shifting my focus made all
the difference. With God's help I was able to begin the work—and
beginning was the hardest part.

I've learned how various aspects of a task can intimidate us to the point where we will put it off as long as we can. The mere size of a task can frighten us and literally paralyze us with fear. We can also feel intimidated by any risks involved with the job or any pressures associated with it. I know from experience how a fear of failure can immobilize us and hinder our productivity. Whatever the cause of our fear or dread, we don't have to let our fears control us. We can seek God in prayer and ask Him to help us focus on taking the first step involved with our task. If we refuse to focus on more than one step at a time, we'll be able to move ahead and begin to make progress. All the Lord wants is to see us make an effort to cooperate with Him in accomplishing our task. Once we demonstrate to Him that we're willing to take the first step, His grace will be there as we need it to take each successive step. I don't stop praying once I've actually begun a task. I keep praying all the way through, being sure to thank and praise Him for His continued help. I always find that this not only helps me to complete the task, but to do it with more joy and satisfaction than I anticipated. Proverbs 16:3 TLB says, "Commit everything you do to the Lord. Trust Him to help you do it and He will." As we ask in faith for God's involvement in all that we do, He rewards us with the motivation, energy, and skill we need to get the job done successfully. If you are a child of God, you've been equipped with Holy Spirit power to accomplish even difficult

LIVE ON PURPOSE TODAY

Today is your day! What is that task or assignment that you've put off? Promise yourself right now that before the sun sets, you'll take a step—even if a small step— toward your goal.

and "impossible" tasks with a holy ease and joy. So when you've got a daunting task before you, take heart from the verses we read at the beginning that David spoke to his son, Solomon, when he was faced with the awesome task of building the temple of God. Don't be intimidated by the size or pressures of the task, but remember that God is with you and He will help you every step of the way!

PRAYER

Lord, when I'm feeling discouraged and frightened about a task before me, show me how to focus on You instead of my fears. Help me to concentrate on taking one step at a time, and help me to cooperate with You to accomplish the work with a holy ease and joy. Thank You, Lord, that because You're with me, I shall succeed in all my undertakings! (2 Kings 18:7 TLB.)

Believe and See His Glory

Against all hope, Abraham in hope believed and so became the father of many nations, just as it had been said to him, "So shall your offspring be." Without weakening in his faith, he faced the fact that his body was as good as dead—since he was about a hundred years old—and that Sarah's womb was also dead. Yet he did not waver through unbelief regarding the promise of God, but was strengthened in his faith and gave glory to God, being fully persuaded that God had power to do what he had promised.

ROMANS 4:18-21

These verses are a great encouragement to those of us who have ever had to endure long periods of waiting before we saw the fulfillment of God's promises to us. The emphasis here is upon the fact that Abraham's situation was completely hopeless. Yet he believed God's promise to give him a son in his old age. It was many years before God fulfilled this promise to Abraham, and he made some mistakes during those years. Still, these verses don't mention Abraham's doubts, but focus instead on his faith. That fact should encourage us, too. Though we may struggle with our own doubts from time to time, if we hold on to God's promises, we will receive our reward just as Abraham did.

If you are not feeling very hopeful today that God's promises to you will ever come to pass, I urge you to hold on to your faith. Look at these verses in Hebrews 10:35-36 NLT: "Do not throw away this confident trust in the Lord, no matter what happens. Remember the great reward it brings you! Patient endurance is what you need now, so you will continue to do God's will. Then you will receive all that He has promised." If you throw your faith

LIVE ON PURPOSE TODAY

Whether you feel like it or not, whether your faith is on the brink of faltering or you are standing strong, lift your hands even now and offer thanksgiving and praise to the One who always keeps His promise of victory to those who trust Him.

away before God fulfills His promises to you, you will never receive the reward He has waiting for you. Ask the Lord to give you the patience and endurance you need to stand strong, then do your part by hanging in there when the going gets tough. Hebrews 6:12 TLB says, "Be anxious to follow the example of those who receive all that God has promised them because of their strong faith and patience." Follow Abraham's example and receive all that the Lord has promised you. Not only will you be blessed, but God will be glorified through you, and then you can be an example to someone else whose faith is faltering. The Living Bible says that Abraham "praised God for this blessing even before it happened." If you'll begin thanking God right now for the fulfillment of those promises that look like they'll never come to pass, your faith will grow by leaps and bounds and you will delight the heart of God. Take heart from this precious verse in 2 Timothy 2:13 TLB: "Even when we are too weak to have any faith left, he remains faithful to us and will help us, for he cannot disown us who are part of himself, and he will always carry out his promises to us"!

PRAYER

Lord, whenever I'm tempted to doubt Your promises, increase my faith and give me the patience I need to stand strong. Help me to take my eyes off my circumstances and rest them on Your promises. Thank You for enabling me to receive all that You have promised!

Needs Vs. Wants

*You do not have, because you do not ask God. When you ask,
you do not receive, because you ask with wrong motives....*

JAMES 4:2,3

O ne day, after my son made a remark about the pitiful condition of our dining room set, I mentioned to him that I
had been praying for a new one. He promptly informed
me that new dining room furniture was not a need, and that I
shouldn't ask God to replace it for me. At first his comments convicted me and made me feel guilty about my petitions. Then I
went to the Lord in prayer and asked Him to give me His view on
the situation. Immediately, some of my favorite verses came to
mind: "Delight yourself in the Lord and he will give you the
desires of your heart" (Ps. 37:4). "He fulfills the desires of those
who fear him" (Ps. 145:19). "Ask and you will receive, and your
joy will be complete" (John 16:24). God reassured me that He
wants to fulfill our needs and our desires, and it isn't our job to
figure out which is which.

Look at the verses above again in James 4. God says there
are some blessings we don't have simply because we didn't ask
Him for them. Many times it doesn't even occur to us to ask God
for certain things that He is eager to give us—things that He may
never allow us to have if we don't seek Him for them. It never
even occurred to my son to pray for new furniture. Thank God I
didn't have the same attitude he did. These same verses reveal
that if we ask for things with the wrong motives, God will not

LIVE ON PURPOSE TODAY

Take inventory today of
your surroundings and decide
what is most important for
you to trust God for. Then
with a heart centered on
Him—and full of faith—
go to the Lord in prayer.

grant them to us. Why did I want a new dining room set? It wasn't because I wanted to show off to my friends and family. It was because my old set was literally falling apart, and it was uncomfortable for my guests, as well as an embarrassment to me. I have new dining room furniture now, and I appreciate it tremendously because I asked God for it and waited on His timing. These days I have an old car. How many times does it have to break down before I can consider it a "need" and ask God for a newer one? I don't worry about that anymore. I just say, "Lord, I'd like a newer car, but I thank You for the one I have." I feel free to ask God for the desires of my heart, because I love Him with all my heart. I ask for things with the right motives, and I'm willing to wait on God's timing. I can live without nice things. But I can't live without God. With that kind of attitude, I can ask God for the desires of my heart. And so can you.

PRAYER

Lord, teach me how to ask You for all the things You want me to enjoy in this life. Help me to wait on Your perfect timing. Give me a heart that always asks with the right motives. Remind me that even though nice things are desirable, I can live without them. Thank You that You take great pleasure in blessing Your servants! (Ps. 35:27.)

The Difference That Trust Makes

Surely this is our God; we trusted in him, and
he saved us. This is the Lord, we trusted in him;
let us rejoice and be glad in his salvation.

ISAIAH 25:9

As long as we've been married, my husband, Joe, has always worked two or three jobs. That's why it was such a shock to us when he got laid off from his full-time job a couple of years ago. The company which had employed him for 18 years was closing its doors, and even though he had a year's notice, when his last day of work finally came, he still didn't know what to do about his job situation. The following weeks of unemployment were extremely hard on my husband. He tried to keep busy doing tasks around our house, and he regularly contacted employment agencies and searched for job openings in the newspaper and on the Internet. Still, God gave no indication that He was opening a door of opportunity for my husband anytime soon, even though we were praying and standing on His Word. I really became concerned when Joe's anxiety over his joblessness began interfering with his sleep. In all our years of marriage, I had never known my husband to have a problem with sleeping. I tried to encourage and comfort my husband by telling him, "You could get a phone call at any moment that will radically change your whole situation!" And I meant it. I tried to get my husband to remain hopeful. I knew it was vital to his well-being. After six weeks of being jobless, Joe received a call from a major communications company, offering him almost twice the salary he was earning at his previous job. It would be a new field of work for him, and he knew the job might only be temporary, but he was pretty sure that it was God's will for him to accept it, so he did.

About one year later my husband was laid off from his new job. Even though he knew the job was most likely only temporary, he had hoped the Lord would spare him from having to endure another period of joblessness. It didn't happen. Once again, Joe was without a steady full-time job, and he had no idea where he would find another one. But this time things were different. Even though my husband would experience brief periods of restlessness, overall, he was sustained by an indescribable peace. Because he had experienced for himself the faithfulness of God the first time he lost his job, he was able to face this newest challenge with a Spirit-given confidence, peace, and strength. The weeks of waiting went by more quickly this time, and the Lord made a way for Joe to find employment at an affiliate of his old company, where he would be doing the kind of work he had done in the past—work he felt the most confident doing. Though the salary was well below his temporary communications job, he

LIVE ON PURPOSE TODAY

Whatever your need, go to the Word of God today and find three Scriptures that cover your case and promise that your heavenly Father will meet your need. Keep those Scriptures very close by—in your heart and in your mouth.

was reinstated with all his original vacation time, health benefits, and seniority—advantages that his previous job had lacked.

Because of these experiences, my husband gained a victory and an intimate knowledge of God's faithfulness that no one can take away from him. He discovered how we can wake up with a problem one day and, by the end of the day, be free from it. He also discovered how trusting God and remaining expectant can keep God's peace and joy flowing in our lives, making our periods of waiting more enjoyable and far less stressful. The Lord knows that we will be spending a good portion of our lives waiting on Him. Because of that, He has made a way for us to wait with peace and joy. But it's up to us to take hold of these gifts by placing our trust in Him and refusing to live in fear and doubt. If you are in a place of uncertainty right now, hoping for God's direction and deliverance, dare to put your trust in Him and to wait expectantly for Him to act on your behalf. Give Him the opportunity to prove to you that He is true to His Word which promises, "The Lord is good, a refuge in times of trouble. He cares for those who trust in him"! (Nah. 1:7).

PRAYER

Lord, in times of trouble and uncertainty, help me to trust You with all my heart. When I'm tempted to doubt or become fearful, remind me of how these attitudes can rob me of peace and joy. Thank You that "None of those who have faith in God will ever be disgraced for trusting Him"! (Ps. 25:3 TLB).

Making Way for the New

Forget the former things; do not dwell on the past. See, I am doing a new thing! Now it springs up; do you not perceive it?

ISAIAH 43:18,19

Until recently, I was using a wonderful old pocketbook that I enjoyed for more than three years. I've always been fussy about my purses, and because of that, it's always been difficult for me to find ones that really suited my needs. The past year or so, my dependable old pocketbook was beginning to fade and look shabby. My husband began urging me to buy a new one. He'd say, "Don't you think it's about time that you put that old purse aside and got a new one?" He'd even help me look for one whenever we'd be out shopping. I made some halfhearted efforts to search for a new purse, just to quiet my husband. But the truth was that I was satisfied and comfortable with my old purse, and my heart just wasn't in replacing it. A few weeks ago I was at a family gathering, when I reached into my purse, and it literally fell apart in my hands. I became upset and handed it to my husband, demanding that he fix it immediately. I silently pleaded with God to make a way for my beloved purse to be restored. Then came the bad news. "This purse can't be repaired. You're just going to have to buy a new one," my husband said. I was heartbroken. Didn't he know how hard it would be for me to replace that purse? Didn't he know how much that purse meant to me, and all that I had invested in it? I finally realized that I had no choice but to start searching for a new purse in earnest. At first I was totally resistant to the idea, but after I prayed and committed the matter to the Lord, I was able to let go of my stubbornness and disappointment. That's when God led me to a wonderful new purse that turned out to be even better than my old one. Every day I thank Him for my new purse and for allowing my old one to be beyond repair so that I could receive the new one He had waiting for me.

The Lord used this experience to teach me some valuable lessons. I learned once again that even though God may have wonderful new experiences and blessings up ahead for us, we will never be able to receive them until we let go of some of the things we are clinging to in the present. The Bible says, "Forget the former things; do not dwell on the past. See, I am doing a new thing! Now it springs up; do you not perceive it?" (Isa. 43:18,19). I like the way The Living Bible says, "Forget all that—it is nothing compared to what I'm going to do!" Our God is a God of progress and improvement. When He is prodding us to let go of something, you can bet it's because He has something better for us waiting up ahead. Those of you who have walked with the Lord for many years know from personal experience how true this is. Because letting go of things we feel comfortable with can

LIVE ON PURPOSE TODAY

Ask yourself an important question: Is there an area where you're holding on so tightly to the past that your knuckles are white? If you must answer yes, pry yourself loose in prayer today and make ready for good things ahead.

be a painful process, we often put it off until something happens to force us to let go. Then we panic and feel lost and forsaken. If we will look at these endings as new beginnings, we will open the door for God to do something new and wonderful in our lives. It all begins with committing everything we have and all that we are to the Lord each day, asking Him to give us the wisdom and strength we need to follow His perfect will, even when it means letting go of something we are desperately holding on to. The apostle Paul wrote, "But one thing I do: forgetting what lies behind and reaching forward to what lies ahead, I press on toward the goal for the prize of the upward call of God in Christ Jesus" (Phil. 3:13,14 NASB). Paul knew that his Lord was always calling him "upward," not downward. He knew that whenever God asked him to leave something behind, it was for his own good, as well as for the Lord's glory. And because of this apostle's willingness to make God-inspired sacrifices, he was mightily used of God. My prayer for you today is that you won't shy away from letting go of the things in your life that would keep you from God's best, but that you'll do whatever it takes to receive all the good things He has in store for you!

PRAYER

Lord, please reveal to me how this message might apply to my life today. Help me to make way for the new things You want to do in my life, by letting go of the old things You want me to leave behind. I want to receive all the good things You have in store for me, and I want to be mightily used by You. Thank You that as I "forget the former things," You'll do new and wonderful things in my life!

Praying God's Will

"This is the confidence we have in approaching God:
that if we ask anything according to his will, he hears us.
And if we know that he hears us—whatever we ask—
we know that we have what we asked of him."

1 JOHN 5:14,15

In these verses, the apostle John assures us that we can have "confidence" in prayer. The key, he says, is praying in line with God's will. I have found that the best place to start in praying according to the will of God is with His Word. No matter what we are facing, God has instructions, insights, and promises that apply to our situation. The Bible reveals God's will concerning our relationships, health, finances, education, vocation, and everything else pertaining to our lives here on earth. It's up to us to search out the verses that relate to our situation and ask the Lord how we can apply them. Jesus said, "If ye abide in Me, and My words abide in you, ye shall ask what ye will, and it shall be done unto you" (John 15:7 KJV). It is in knowing and believing God's Word that our hearts and minds are transformed, and our wills become aligned with God's. We are then able to pray the prayers of God's own heart, and as a result, we are assured of the answer to our prayers. Romans 12:2 NLT says, "Don't copy the behavior and customs of this world, but let God transform you into a new person by changing the way you think. Then you will know what God wants you to do, and you will know how good and pleasing and perfect his will really is." In this verse, the apostle Paul urges us to allow God to renew our minds so that we will be able to prove what His perfect will is. We can cooperate with God's plan to transform our thinking by studying, believing, and meditating on His Word. In this way, we will reprogram our minds with God's truth and leave behind the worldly, negative thinking which would cause us to pray ineffectively and with little or no results.

Not only has God given us His Word to help us pray effectively, but He has also given us His Spirit. Romans 8:26 NLT says, "The Holy Spirit helps us in our distress. For we don't even know what we should pray for, nor how we should pray. But the Holy Spirit prays for us." And the next verse tells us, "The Spirit pleads for us believers in harmony with God's own will." God knows there will be times when we won't know how to pray correctly, and He has made special provision for us in those times through His Spirit. We don't have to be at the mercy of our emotions in trying times, but we can call upon God and ask Him to help us pray the prayers of His own heart through His Spirit. The Bible is a source of wonderful, Spirit-given prayers we can apply to our lives and situations. As believers we have the privilege—and often the obligation—to pray the same prayers that Jesus, Paul, and David did for ourselves and others. And no matter what comes our way, we can rest assured

LIVE ON PURPOSE TODAY

The Spirit of God inspired the apostle Paul to pray some mighty prayers—prayers that are also important for you to pray. Open your Bible now to Ephesians 1:15-23, Ephesians 3:13-21, Philippians 1:9-11, and Colossians 1:9-11, and pray these inspired prayers inserting your name. They will bless you abundantly!

that God has promises in His Word that we can pray and stand on for our deliverance and victory. If we go to God with our troubles and concerns and ask Him for a promise of our very own to claim, He will show it to us. Then it's up to us to lay hold of that promise by faith and stand on it until our answer comes. And let's never forget that God sees our hearts. If we have a sincere desire to please Him, and we trust that He always wants the best for us, we can pray the way we feel "led" to. Even if we "miss" God, He will redirect us and turn our hearts toward His will, simply because He knows we love Him. It's my prayer that you would begin praying with confidence and discover the joy of being in partnership with God to see His will come to pass in your life and in this earth.

PRAYER

Lord, teach me to pray the prayers of Your heart for myself and others in every situation. May the desires of my heart never be in conflict with the desires of Yours. Give me a love for Your Word and help me to use it to renew my mind. Thank You that in times of uncertainty, I can depend on Your Holy Spirit to help me pray!

Overlooked and Unappreciated

Then the king said to Zadok, "Take the ark of God back into the city. If I find favor in the Lord's eyes, He will bring me back and let me see it and His dwelling place again. But if He says, 'I am not pleased with you,' then I am ready; let Him do to me whatever seems good to Him."

2 SAMUEL 15:25,26

These words of King David have been a profound inspiration to me at times when I've felt overlooked, passed over, or treated unfairly. David is considered by many to be the most victorious warrior of all time, and yet when his own son, Absalom, conspires against him to steal his throne, instead of retaliating, he commits himself to God and His sense of justice. He doesn't whine, complain, or feel sorry for himself. He just basically says, "Lord, I put myself in Your hands. Do with me whatever You think is right. I trust You." And David's attitude was a Christlike one, according to the Scripture which says, "When [Jesus] suffered, He did not threaten to get even. He left His case in the hands of God, who always judges fairly" (1 Peter 2:23 NLT). As it turned out, the Lord did restore David to his throne, and I believe that his unwavering trust in God was the main reason why.

Sooner or later all of us will experience the pain and disappointment of having our efforts ignored, minimized, or criticized by others. I believe that how we respond in times like these not only indicates our level of spiritual maturity, but also determines our outcome. One thing that helps me is remembering that whatever we do should be done "unto the Lord." The apostle Paul wrote, "Work hard and cheerfully at all you do, just as though you were working for the Lord and not merely for your masters, remembering that it is the Lord Christ who is going to pay you, giving you your full portion of all He owns. He is the one you are really working for" (Col. 3:23,24 TLB). These verses clearly convey the perspective we should have in all we do. If we focus on pleasing God and doing our best in everything, we won't be so resentful, hurt, or discouraged when others don't appreciate or reward our efforts. Instead, we can rest secure in the knowledge that God is fully aware of all we do, and He will see that we get the recognition and reward we deserve in His perfect way and timing. Even if those we are working for are continually unreasonable or unfair, we can take heart from God's reassurance that "nothing can hinder the Lord" (1 Sam. 14:6 NLT). There may be times when it looks like others are succeeding in delaying or preventing our progress, but the truth is that when God decides to bless and promote His people, no person on earth and no devil in hell can stop Him. If you can relate to this message today, let me encourage you to get your eyes off other people and get them squarely on God. Work hard and do your best in all you do, trusting that the Lord Himself will honor you for it, even if others don't. Let your declaration of faith be the

LIVE ON PURPOSE TODAY

When you're tempted to feel overlooked and unappreciated, encourage yourself with the Scriptures above. Read them, meditate upon them, and be enlivened by them!

psalmist's—"You will give me greater honor than before, and turn again and comfort me"! (Ps. 71:22 TLB).

PRAYER

Lord, I believe that true honor and promotion come from You.
(Ps. 75:6,7 TLB.) When my efforts are overlooked or unappreciated,
I ask that You help me to respond in a Christlike manner.
Strengthen me to resist becoming angry, resentful, frustrated, or
discouraged. Show me how to pray for those who treat me unfairly.
Thank You that as I depend on You for justice and reward, You
will lift me up and exalt me at the proper time! (1 Peter 5:6.)

Our Giving God

*He who did not withhold or spare [even] His own Son but
gave Him up for us all, will He not also with Him
freely and graciously give us all [other] things?*

ROMANS 8:32 AMP

When my son John was in college a few years ago, he was in desperate need of a car. My husband, Joe, was driving a very old vehicle at the time, and he told John that as soon as he could find a newer car for himself, he would give our son the one he was currently driving. Shortly afterwards we were delighted to discover that one of my sisters was selling her car, and she would be more than happy to let Joe buy it. Right before we were to pick up my sister's car, my older son, Joseph's, car broke down. When he brought it to be fixed, he was told that because of the age and condition of the car, it wasn't worth repairing. Because Joseph was on his own and had a full-time job, my husband and I felt compelled to offer him the car meant for John. Naturally, John was bitterly disappointed. He had already told all of his friends about his "new" car, and he had his heart set on it. I told him to do his best, with God's help, to maintain a good attitude about the matter so that the Lord would work everything out for his good in the long run. As it turned out, John didn't harbor any ill feelings toward us or his brother, and we all prayed that God would honor and reward him for his Christlike attitude. Some weeks later my husband found an especially good deal on a new car, and he happily presented my sister's old car to John. Though John had missed out on the vehicle that was originally intended for him, he wound up with a newer and nicer car—with more options than he ever expected.

This experience is just another reminder to us that God is a giver, not a taker. The Bible says that "God so loved the world that He *gave...*" (John 3:16). And Romans 8:32 says, "He who did not spare His own Son, but gave Him up for us all—how will He not also, along with Him, graciously give us all things?" When we suffer a loss of some kind, why are we so quick to believe that God wants to rob us of something good? I'm not saying that every time we lose something or suffer disappointment we should be jumping for joy. Life is hard and it's filled with losses and disappointments, and there will be times when we need to cry and feel sad for a while. But I do believe that how we view God and His dealings with us during these times will have an impact on our ultimate outcome. When things don't go our way, when our expectations aren't fulfilled, we can be tempted to get angry at God or other people. We can also be tempted to drown in self-pity, and to whine and complain about the injustices of life. But that will do us no good at all. What *will* do us good is to have a different mindset. Suppose when my son John found out that my husband and I were giving the car meant for him to his brother instead, he threw a fit and became bitter and resentful toward us and our other son. Do you really think that God would have honored that kind of behavior by rewarding him with an even better vehicle? I sincerely doubt it. The Bible clearly states that we reap what we sow (Gal. 6:7), and bitter feelings and attitudes always yield a bitter harvest.

LIVE ON PURPOSE TODAY

Take a few moments to check your heart and make sure that your attitudes are right before the Lord. If not, make a few adjustments. Then heed the words of Psalm 84—trust in God and get happy!

Fortunately, John chose to trust in God's good and giving nature, and because of that, he was able to resist responding to his disappointment with anger or resentment, clearing the way for the Lord to richly reward him.

Perhaps a good illustration is one I heard long ago from a godly man. Imagine God asking you to give Him twenty dollars. That's a lot of money to you, so you hesitate, but then finally give in and hand it over to Him. In return, He gives you a hundred dollar bill. Well, if you had known in advance that He was going to give you much more than what you gave up, you would have gladly handed over that twenty dollars. But you *didn't* know. And most of the time, God doesn't reveal to us in advance that He is asking us to give up one thing so that He can give us something even better in return. That's exactly why the Bible talks so much about the importance of trusting God. If we believe that God is good, just, and generous—that He's a giver and not a taker—we will handle the losses and disappointments that come our way with a better attitude, and God will richly reward us in the end. The next time you're faced with a situation like my son's, refuse to see the Lord as anything but the loving, giving God that He is. And rest on His precious promise that says, "No good thing will the Lord withhold from those who do what is right. O Lord Almighty, happy are those who trust in You!" (Ps. 84:11,12 NLT).

PRAYER

Lord, forgive me for the times I suffered a loss or disappointment and reacted badly about it. From now on, teach me to see these experiences as tests, and help me to pass them with a holy ease and joy so that I can receive all the promotions, victories, and blessings You have in store for me. Thank You for helping me to see You as You really are—a good and gracious God who loves to give to His children!

God Cares About the Details

{ *God cares, cares right down to the last detail.* }

JAMES 5:11 MESSAGE

Recently, it was my friend Peggy's birthday, and I prayed and asked the Lord how I could bless her. I thought of buying her a copy of one of the books I have that I've really enjoyed. But when I got to the store, I felt led to purchase an entirely different book for her instead. I selected a beautiful card with warm sentiments and added some of my own. When I prayed about anything else I could add to her birthday package, it seemed as if the Lord was leading me to put some money in it. My mind immediately thought, *No way. What will she think?* But in the end, I included the money and prayed I was doing the right thing. I found out a few days later that the day my package arrived, Peggy had had a rough day at work. As she drove home that evening, she thought of treating herself to a manicure but quickly gave up the idea when she remembered her many recent expenditures. When she opened my package and discovered the money in her card, she rejoiced and headed straight for the beauty salon with her new book in hand. As it turned out, the book I gave her was filled with just the kind of inspirational stories that delight and encourage her heart.

One of the things I appreciate most about Peggy is that she believes, as I do, that God cares about all the little details of our lives. I know that if I want someone to agree in prayer with me about even the smallest matters concerning me or my family, I can count on Peggy. And I am always amazed at how the Lord continually honors our prayers for even the "small stuff." It saddens me to hear so many believers say things like—"You actually bother God with that kind of stuff?"—whenever they find out that someone is seeking the Lord about something "unimportant." Not only are they missing out on some awesome blessings, but they will never enjoy the depth of intimacy that the Lord longs to share with them. I love the fact that I can consult God when I'm planning on buying a gift for someone. My experience with buying Peggy's gift gave me a new reassurance that this is fact and not fiction. The Lord knows that we are in a constant battle against good and evil in this world, and He's aware of how weary we can get. He longs to encourage us regularly with countless little blessings, as well as with big ones. These little encouragements can give us the lift we need to keep pressing on to the victory when we've been tempted to lose heart. Sometimes I feel like I need a special touch from God, so I pray something like, "Lord, do something new and wonderful in my life!" I may not even know what it is that I want Him to do, but He knows, and He never disappoints me. Don't let anyone tell you that God doesn't care about the little details of your life. There are plenty of believers who are constantly proving otherwise, and I'm one of them. My friend Peggy is another. Jesus said, "Ask, using my name, and you will receive, and your cup of joy will overflow" (John 16:24 TLB). Don't wait a minute longer.

LIVE ON PURPOSE TODAY

Take a few moments to survey your life and pinpoint anything you previously thought too small to take to the Lord. If you find something, hand it over to Him. God will do the caring!

Take the Lord up on His offer today, and let Him prove to you once again that He's true to His Word. May this precious promise from God encourage your heart today: "The steps of the godly are directed by the Lord. He delights in every detail of their lives"! (Ps. 37:23 NLT).

PRAYER

Lord, help me to never buy into that lie that says You aren't interested in the little details of my life. Give me a new awareness of just how much You want to be involved in everything that concerns me. Teach me how to pray about the "small stuff," and help me to be sensitive to Your Spirit's leading. Thank You that I will really know You then as I never have before! (Hosea 2:20 TLB.)

Dating: One Mom's Perspective

> "Don't copy the behavior and customs of this world, but let God transform you into a new person by changing the way you think. Then you will know what God wants you to do, and you will know how good and pleasing and perfect His will really is."
>
> ROMANS 12:2 NLT

I often hear from people—both parents and children alike—who ask my opinion on dating from a Christian perspective. I don't profess to be an expert by any means, but I do often share with them some of my own experiences as a parent. I tell them candidly that I did not allow my own sons to date until they were 18 years old. I came to this decision after much prayer, as well as the realization that I didn't want to automatically accept the world's view on dating. I recalled the fact that my father always regretted allowing my sisters and me to enter the "dating scene" when we were only 16 years of age, and as I looked back, I understood the basis for his regrets. All of us had experienced heartbreak and misery that we could have been spared if we had just waited for God's will and timing where our relationships were concerned. When I finally made my decision about my sons, I began hearing disturbing warnings from other parents. Some said that I was robbing my children of healthy, valuable experiences that would benefit them later in life. Many said that my kids were "missing out." I must admit that there were times when I wavered and wondered if I was being unreasonable or legalistic. It was especially difficult when I saw my sons struggling with feeling left out of groups of their peers that were all couples. But by the grace of God, we all got through it, and I believe to this day that I made the right decision in making them wait.

My older son, Joseph, has been married the last two years to a wonderful young lady named Miriam, whom he met through his college Bible club. They met when they were both 18 years old, and they married after knowing each other for five years. Joseph and Miriam are deeply committed to each other, and I believe they have many happily married years ahead of them. In only a matter of months, my younger son, John, will be marrying Amy, a sweet young lady whom he met through his high school Bible club. By the time that John and Amy walk down the aisle together, they will have been together for five years. Both Amy and Miriam are godly young women and delightful additions to our family. And both are totally devoted to my sons. I don't bring all this up to boast or to tell you what you should do, but to give you an example of just how wrong some of the world's views on dating and child rearing can be. Yes, it's certainly true that my kids "missed out." They missed out on untold amounts of misery and heartbreak, as well as all the far-reaching, negative consequences of being involved with relationships that were out of God's will and timing for them. And while it was difficult for my family to take an unpopular stand and to wait for what we

LIVE ON PURPOSE TODAY

Establish three Bible-inspired goals today that will better enable you to resemble your Lord and not the world. Write down your goals and keep them centered in your heart.

believed was the Lord's timing, He rewarded us by blessing my sons with the perfect mates, without them having to go through a string of "imperfect" ones.

If you are a parent or a single person dealing with one side or another of this issue, let me encourage you today to give less attention to the world's ideas and standards for dating relationships, and more attention to the Lord's. He alone knows what's best for us, and if you jump ahead of His perfect plan and timing in this area, you could very well delay or miss out on His best for you, or your children. Today, ask the Lord to give you some new attitudes so that you'll be able to see things His way from now on. And receive all the good things He has in store for you and yours!

PRAYER

Lord, forgive me for the times I've followed the ways of the world instead of Your ways. Grant that I may be "constantly renewed in the spirit of my mind—having a fresh mental and spiritual attitude," so that I may obey You in every area and reap all the blessings You have for me and mine (Eph. 4:23 AMP). I pray that my relationships will be all that You want them to be, and only what You want them to be!

Pour On the Love

He has been punished enough by your united disapproval.
Now it is time to forgive him and comfort him. Otherwise he may
become so bitter and discouraged that he won't be able to recover.
Please show him now that you still do love him very much.

2 CORINTHIANS 2:6-8 TLB

The Lord gave me these verses a few years ago, after my husband and I asked our older son, Joseph, to leave our home because of his rebelliousness. We and our younger son, John, were indeed united in our disapproval of Joseph's destructive and disruptive behavior. We knew his conduct was wrong and that it was a threat to our family's well-being. And we were often hurt and bewildered by Joseph's open hostility toward us. As a result, I believe we often acted even worse than he did. What began as correction and rebuke on our part eventually turned into bitter criticism and condemnation. Needless to say, our tactics often did more harm than good, and the strife and division in our family escalated. When the Lord brought these verses to my attention, I felt convicted and ashamed. I turned to God in repentance and asked Him to help me forgive my son so that I could give him the love, acceptance, and comfort he desperately needed. The Lord answered that prayer by changing my heart and bringing healing to my family.

In 1 Corinthians 5:5 TLB, the apostle Paul talks about how sometimes it's necessary for us to "cast out" someone "from the fellowship" and "into Satan's hands to punish him, in the hope that his soul will be saved when our Lord Jesus Christ returns." Paul says this because he knows that allowing people to experience the natural consequences of their misdeeds is an effective means of discipline. As painful as it was for my husband and me to turn our son out of our home, we knew it was the only way to force him to become accountable for his actions. It also forced him to rely less on his family and more on God for his provision and protection. Paul also voices his concerns about the offender's influence on the fellowship as a whole: "Don't you realize that if even one person is allowed to go on sinning, soon all will be affected?" (1 Cor. 5:6 TLB). My husband and I knew that if we continued to tolerate our son's open rebellion against us and God, we would be risking the spiritual health of our younger son and our family as a whole. But just as there is a time to confront a sinner, there is also a time to "forgive and comfort him" so that "he won't become so bitter and discouraged that he won't be able to recover" (2 Cor. 2:7 TLB). Confronting and disciplining sinners should be for the purpose of their restoration, not their ruin. As Paul states, "A further reason for forgiveness is to keep from being outsmarted by Satan; for we know what he is trying to do" (2 Cor. 2:11 TLB). Refusing to forgive a sinner at the

LIVE ON PURPOSE TODAY

Inspect your heart today, looking for those with whom you should disassociate or better associate. Is there someone you should draw away from until his or her path aligns with the Lord's? Or is there someone in need of you to pour on the love?

proper time can allow the devil to take advantage of the discord in the fellowship or family, creating greater division and dissension.

The Scriptures instruct us exactly how God expects us to confront and correct others: "If a Christian is overcome by some sin, you who are godly should gently and humbly help him back onto the right path, remembering that next time it might be one of you who is in the wrong" (Gal. 6:1 TLB). If necessary discipline is administered in gentleness and humility, with love as the motivation, God's presence and power will be there to make it as effective as the offender allows. Our son never did turn to us in remorse and repentance, but the Lord knew it was time for us to "pour on the love" just the same (2 Cor. 2:8 MESSAGE). And because we obeyed His leading, our family was restored and God was glorified. Of course, not all situations like these can have a happy ending. Believers are called to put God first in their lives, and sometimes that creates lasting conflict between us and others, even where family members are concerned. (Luke 12:51-53.) But it's our responsibility to discover God's will in these matters, and to do what pleases and glorifies Him most. (Eph. 5:10.)

PRAYER

Lord, remind me that there's a time to confront and a time to comfort, and help me to know which principle to apply when. Make me steadfast in faithfulness to You and Your Word, but make me loving and forgiving, too. Thank You that as I am sensitive and obedient to Your leading, my relationships will please and glorify You!

Do You Want To Get Well?

*When Jesus saw him lying there and learned that
he had been in this condition for a long time,
He asked him, "Do you want to get well?"*

JOHN 5:6

Many times I've read the above words by Jesus and thought to myself, *Who wouldn't want to get well if they were hurting in some way?* That question was answered for me recently when I was having a phone conversation with a lady from my church. She was going through a very difficult time in her life, and she was having a hard time dealing with all the injustices that were being heaped upon her, seemingly all at one time. As we chatted, it became clear to me that she was harboring a lot of bitterness and resentment toward all the people she felt had done her wrong. When I reminded her that Jesus has commanded us to forgive those who offend us, she insisted that she had a right to be resentful, and that she had no intention of forgiving those who hurt her. When I suggested that there might be a connection between her recent health problems and her feelings of resentment, she said she didn't care. She also confessed that she was angry with God, and that her troubles were not drawing her closer to Him, but only further away. I decided then to drop the subject and to commit myself to pray for her in a more earnest manner from then on.

Why is it that some people become bitter when they go through hard times, while others become better? Perhaps part of the answer lies in an old saying that still rings true today: "The same hot water that hardens an egg, softens a carrot." We don't always have a choice about what happens to us, but we do have the power to choose how we will respond to the difficulties that come our way. Because this woman chose to withhold forgiveness from those who wounded her, she had also made the choice to forfeit the valuable help the Lord would have given her if she had only obeyed Him. Jesus said, "If you do not forgive men their sins, your Father will not forgive your sins" (Matt. 6:15). Unforgiveness is serious business in God's eyes, and we need to view it the same way and act accordingly. Fortunately, we don't have to forgive others in our own strength. We have the Holy Spirit pouring the God-kind of love into our hearts as we walk with Him daily. (Rom. 5:5.) The apostle Paul warns us that withholding forgiveness from others can open the door to satanic attack. (Eph. 4:26-28.) Maybe this woman's recent health problems weren't a direct result of her resentment, but one thing was certain—her bitterness was hindering her prayers, including her prayers for healing. In at least two places in the Gospels, Jesus reveals a link between the effectiveness of our prayers and our obligation to forgive others. (Matt. 6:14,15; Mark 11:25.)

LIVE ON PURPOSE TODAY

Is there anyone anywhere whom you do not forgive? If your answer is yes, go to the Lord in prayer even now and forgive the person as an act of your will. The time is right to make things right.

Perhaps the Lord is asking you today, "Do you want to get well?" No matter what you've been through or how many emotional scars you've built up over the years, healing and restoration are available to you. All you need to do is stop focusing on your wounds and begin focusing on the cure. There is no pain, injury, or hurt that the love of God cannot heal. I'm living proof of that, and so are many others. Ask the Lord to search your heart and reveal to you who it is you need to forgive. Then leave all your bitterness, resentment, and unforgiveness at the foot of the Cross—and let the healing begin!

PRAYER

Lord, teach me how to forgive others quickly and thoroughly when they hurt me or treat me unfairly. Remind me that You are faithful to right the wrongs in my life, and to heal and comfort me, when I look to You for wisdom and help in these situations. Thank You, Lord, that by Your grace, I will benefit from my troubles and trials, and I will become better instead of bitter!

Nothing Can Hinder
the Lord

Nothing can hinder the Lord.

1 SAMUEL 14:6 NLT

O n one occasion last summer my husband, Joe, had to report to work on a Saturday. I decided to take the ride with him because my sister lived near his office, and he offered to drop me off there on the way. The weather was hot and muggy that day, and since it was his company's policy to turn off the air conditioning on the weekend, Joe was dreading having to work in stifling conditions. I sympathized with him and suggested that he ask the Lord to have his office nice and cool when he arrived there. His reply was something like, "My coworkers told me that the air conditioning has always been off on weekends. It's going to be unbearably hot when I get there." I tried to encourage him to pray about it anyway. "Why don't we ask the Lord to make an exception, and arrange to have the air conditioning left on just for you?" But no matter how I tried, I couldn't get my husband to agree in prayer with me, so I told him that I would pray about it myself, and we left it at that. My silent prayer went something like this: "Lord, I know that it would be an easy thing for You to provide air conditioning for Joe when he arrives at his office today, even if it's never happened before. I'm asking You to do that, Lord, not just so he can work in comfort, but also so that he'll have a new awareness of Your ability and willingness to work wonders on his behalf, even in the seemingly small things that concern him." Shortly after I got to my sister's house Joe called and told me with great excitement and amazement that when he arrived at his workplace, it was wonderfully cool and comfortable. My husband's amazement increased even more when he told the story to his coworkers the following Monday, and they were awestruck.

God used this experience to remind my husband and me of the truth of the verse we just read "Nothing can hinder the Lord." Over the last several years I've discovered that our God is very eager to demonstrate His creative and unlimited power, even in the small matters that concern His children. Yet I constantly encounter stubborn resistance and unbelief from even the most committed Christians who refuse to "stick their necks out" faith-wise and ask God for the extraordinary. Personally, I believe it grieves the heart of God. I have an inspirational saying in my office that reads, "Faith sees the invisible, believes the incredible, receives the impossible." It's a principle I try to live by. I continually ask God for all kinds of "little miracles," and I receive a good percentage of them—not because I deserve to, any more than any other believer does, but because I'm just "crazy" enough to ask for them. James 4:2 says, "You do not have, because you do not ask God." This is an admonition from the Spirit of God for those who complain, criticize, envy, or doubt—but who do not

LIVE ON PURPOSE TODAY

Is there a problem or situation you've tried to handle yourself without even realizing it? Give it now to your unhindered God and allow Him to perfect those things that concern you. (Ps. 138:8.)

ask their willing Creator for help. In chapter 6 of Mark, the Scriptures tell of how Jesus brought His miracle-working power to Nazareth, but "could not do any miracles there" because of the people's "lack of faith" (vv. 5,6). The Bible makes it clear that the people's unbelief actually hindered God's miracle-working power. Jesus said, "According to your faith will it be done to you" (Matt. 9:29). And, "It shall be done for you as you have believed" (Matt. 8:13 AMP). To a great extent, how we use our faith determines the amount of involvement God will have with our daily lives. Faith is our means of connecting with God and His supernatural power. It may help you to think of your faith as a muscle that grows as you exercise it. And just as we can become physically lazy, we can become spiritually lazy, too. Hebrews 6:12 says, "We do not want you to become lazy, but to imitate those who through faith and patience inherit what has been promised." The effort we make is well worth it because each time our prayers are answered, our hearts are encouraged, and we show the unbelieving world that we serve a God who loves to bless and tenderly care for His own. From now on, let us always remember that "nothing can hinder the Lord"—except, perhaps, our lack of faith!

PRAYER

Lord, expand my vision and increase my faith daily.
Help me to never put limits on You. Teach me how to
take more risks with my faith in ways that will bless people
and glorify You. Thank You for being a miracle-working
God, and for working wonders on my behalf! (Joel 2:26.)

Faith for Major Decisions

> *If you are walking in darkness, without a ray of light,*
> *trust in the Lord and rely on your God.*
>
> ISAIAH 50:10 NLT

I was recently faced with a major decision that had me completely petrified. I must admit that whenever I'm faced with the possibility of having to sign a legal document of some kind, my first reaction is sheer terror. My fears are often compounded by well-meaning people around me who take great pains to describe in detail the worst possible scenarios that could befall me. Years ago I might have decided to just forget the whole thing. But these days I'm in the habit of seeking the Lord about every decision I face, so I turned to Him for His perspective on the matter. I told Him that even though I was terrified, I wanted His will above all else, and I asked Him to guide and guard my every step. As the time approached for me to sign on the dotted line, I began pouring my heart out to God, telling Him my fears about trusting the people involved. It was then that I heard Him speak to my heart, "I'm not asking you to trust them. I'm asking you to trust *Me*." Hearing these reassuring words from the Lord calmed my fears and enabled me to settle down and put my trust in Him.

At the same time I was going through this experience, a close friend of mine was faced with a major decision of her own. She was having many of the same misgivings that I was, and she was afraid of making a mistake. I told her that I would pray for her, and I shared with her some things I've learned over the years about following God's lead. After I pray about a situation, if I feel led to take a step, I go ahead and take one. If I sense that God is giving me a "green light," I go ahead and take another step, praying all the way. If the way seems clear, and if everything seems to be falling into place, I continue to take more steps. I have found that there's usually a "flow" present which encourages me to keep going. If things seem stalled—if I sense that God is giving me a "red light"—I pause and wait on Him for further instructions. Because I want God's will and not my own, I ask Him to make me sensitive and obedient to His leading. I also ask Him to give me a sense of peace when I'm on the right track, because Scripture says that we should let the peace of God act as "umpire" in our hearts (Col. 3:15 AMP). This doesn't mean that we won't feel fear or uncertainty if we're in God's will, but that we'll have an unexplainable sense of inner peace in the midst of uncertainty.

LIVE ON PURPOSE TODAY

If you're facing decisions, take a moment to observe the traffic signals in your life. Is the Holy Spirit giving you a red, a green, or a yellow light? Asking and answering that question will bring God-directed clarity on the scene.

My friend is a woman of great faith, and she asked me if I thought that God would be offended if we didn't trust Him for a positive outcome in situations like these. I told her that I think it's a mistake for us to assume that every seemingly wonderful opportunity that comes our way is God's will for us. If we thought that way, we'd be more likely to "kick down doors," and to try to make something happen that the Lord is trying to help us avoid. On the other hand, if we assume a "wait and see" attitude that stems from a lack of faith, we might become too passive and miss out on God's best for us. I believe that if we will ask the Lord to help us find the perfect balance between these two attitudes, and one that is pleasing to Him, He will equip us with everything we need to succeed.

The Bible makes it clear that God is eager to guide us when we turn to Him for help. Even so, there will be times when He will not allow us to have "all our ducks in a row" before He expects us to make a move. These are the times He longs for us to put our trust in Him, so that He can prove His faithfulness to us. Today, may this precious promise from the Lord encourage and reassure you: "Trust in God from the bottom of your heart. Don't try to figure out everything on your own. Listen for God's voice in everything you do, everywhere you go. He's the one who will keep you on track"! (Prov. 3:5,6 MESSAGE).

PRAYER

Lord, when I'm faced with a major decision, help me to turn to You for guidance and to put my trust in You. Give me the courage and the faith to follow Your lead, no matter where it takes me. Help me not to run ahead of You or to lag behind. Remind me to seek You on a daily basis through prayer, praise, and the study of Your Word, so that I'll develop a sensitive and obedient spirit. Thank You, Lord, that when the way is unclear before me, I can trust You to guide and guard my steps!

Turning the Tables
on the Enemy

*As far as I am concerned, God turned
into good what you meant for evil.*

GENESIS 50:20 NLT

Several years ago my husband and I took our sons to a local amusement park. My boys were big baseball fans at the time, and they wanted to use the automatic pitching machines so they could practice their swing. Unfortunately, my son John was hit squarely on his arm with one of the pitches. Immediately, his arm began to swell and discolor ominously. After reporting the injury to the park, we headed for the hospital. On the way there I began claiming Psalm 34:20, which says, "He protects all his bones, not one of them will be broken." When we arrived at the hospital emergency room, we met a mother and her son, who had fallen off his bicycle and injured his arm. Chills ran down my spine when I found out that this boy had not only injured the same arm as my son, but in exactly the same place. The only difference seemed to be that this boy's arm wasn't nearly as swollen or discolored as John's. A short time later my family and I were shocked when the boy came out of the examination room with a cast on his arm, which was indeed broken. Immediately, fear swept over me, and I confess that my faith wavered for a few moments. My initial thought was, *This boy's arm doesn't look half as bad as John's, and his is badly broken, so how can my son's not be broken?!* As I claimed Isaiah 11:3—"He will not judge by what he sees with his eyes or decide by what he hears with his ears"—I felt the peace of God quiet my heart and mind. Moments later doctors examined x-rays of my son's arm and could find no trace of a break—not even the slightest fracture. My family and I still marvel over the miracle of that day, as well as God's faithfulness to His Word.

God used this experience to teach me about some of the strategies Satan employs against believers. When my family and I arrived at the hospital emergency room that day, the devil was counting on me to let go of my faith in God and His Word when I saw the other boy with a cast on his arm. As it turned out, I was tempted to doubt and disbelieve, especially because the feelings of fear I experienced were so sudden and severe. But once I shook off those feelings and took my stand in faith, God honored my decision and increased my strength to stand firm. I can't prove that the outcome of this situation would have been different if I had given in to my fears and doubts, but I believe with all my heart that my "faith decision" made all the difference. It's not unusual for Satan to put people and situations in our path to try to

LIVE ON PURPOSE TODAY

Perhaps the devil has tried to confuse or trick you with symptoms or circumstances. Put him in his place. Decide right this minute that you will walk by faith, and God will back you all the way to victory!

get us to doubt God and His Word. And it's nothing new, either. He's been operating this way since the Garden of Eden. But believers don't have to be ignorant of his tactics. The Bible says that we can gain an awareness of the enemy's schemes that can keep us from getting caught in his snares. (2 Cor. 2:11.) As we seek God daily through prayer, praise, and the reading of His Word, He will equip us with everything we need to defeat Satan and his gang. Then, when the devil tries to set us up for a fall, we can witness our Mighty Warrior King turning the tables on our foes and turning our "curses" into blessings. (Deut. 23:5.) That day at the hospital, Satan tried to use that other boy's injury to discourage and defeat me. Instead, God used it to highlight His miracle-working power. The next time you're faced with a similar situation, take your stand in faith, knowing and declaring—"This is all going to turn out for my good!" (Phil. 1:19 TLB).

PRAYER

Lord, help me to become more aware of Satan's tactics so that I won't be an easy target for his attacks. Teach me how to walk by faith and not by sight. (2 Cor. 5:7.) Show me how to cooperate with You to turn the tables on the devil when he comes against me. Thank You for turning every attack of the enemy into my good!

The Difference Humility Can Make

{ *God sets Himself against the proud, but He shows favor to the humble. So humble yourselves under the mighty power of God, and in His good time, He will honor you.* }

1 PETER 5:5,6 NLT

One day during the past winter season, my husband, Joe, was having a terrible time trying to keep the fire in our coal stove going. It was a bitterly cold day, and the last thing he wanted to do was lose that fire. Joe has always had a natural talent for lighting a coal stove and keeping it burning efficiently, even for weeks at a time. But on this particular day, nothing he did seemed to work. He was getting more frustrated by the hour, and I prayed that God would show him what to do. It got late and I finally went to bed, leaving Joe to keep a close watch on our nearly nonexistent fire. The next morning I asked my husband how the fire was doing. "Great!" he exclaimed. I asked him how he had finally succeeded in his fire-keeping efforts, and he said that at about 3 o'clock in the morning he finally decided to ask God for His help. That's when he got the idea to use a small fan to blow air into the bottom of the stove to get the fire going. It worked like a charm. At that point, Joe asked the Lord why He didn't show him sooner what to do, and he heard the Lord say, "You didn't ask."

My husband's experience reminded me of my children when they were very small. As toddlers, they began showing signs of wanting to become more independent. When I would see them struggling with some small task, like tying their shoes, I would reach down to try to help them with it. They would pull away from me, exclaiming, "I do it!" Then I'd have to stand idly by while they painfully struggled with a task that I could have easily helped them with. It wasn't until the child gave up, totally exasperated, that he would finally come to me and ask for help.

James 4:2 says, "You do not have because you do not ask God." How many things do we struggle with needlessly on a regular basis, simply because we don't ask for God's help? How many blessings do we do without daily, simply because we don't request them from the Lord? It wasn't God's idea for my husband to sit up until 3 o'clock in the morning, nursing a dwindling fire in our coal stove. God knew from the start how Joe could get the fire going. He was just waiting for my husband to humble himself and *ask* Him for help. But either out of ignorance or stubbornness, Joe waited until he was frustrated and irritated before he called on the Lord. The Bible says, "God sets Himself against the proud (the insolent, the overbearing, the disdainful, the presumptuous, the boastful)—[and He opposes, frustrates, and defeats them], but gives grace (favor, blessing) to the humble" (1 Peter 5:5 AMP). It's God's desire to bless us abundantly and to help us become all that He created us to be. But when we insist on depending on ourselves and our own pitiful resources, instead of depending on Him and His grace, He may have to stand idly by until we come to our senses and call on His name. The Lord

LIVE ON PURPOSE TODAY

Consider your agenda for the day, and make sure that you've sought the Lord's help and guidance for each task. Acknowledge to Him one by one that though you are insufficient in yourself, you're well aware that He's more than up to every task.

has awesome plans for the life of every person who puts their trust in Him. But we will never see them come to pass if we don't maintain an attitude of humility before Him. I know Christians who are very talented but insist on using their God-given gifts their own way, so that they never seem to get into the "flow" of the Lord's good plans for them. Though these people have awesome potential, they live frustrated and unfulfilled lives, simply because they refuse to surrender themselves and their own agendas to God. They haven't gotten a revelation of the powerful truths stated in the next verse in this passage of Scripture: "Therefore humble yourselves [demote, lower yourselves in your own estimation] under the mighty hand of God, that in due time He may exalt you" (1 Peter 5:6 AMP). James says it this way: "Humble yourselves [feeling very insignificant] in the presence of the Lord, and He will exalt you [He will lift you up and make your lives significant]" (James 4:10 AMP). Everyone longs to live a life of purpose, meaning, and significance. But these things can never be attained apart from God and His perfect plans for us.

I love the way The Living Bible says, "God gives special blessings to those who are humble" (1 Peter 5:5 TLB). This statement beautifully sums up the difference that humility can make in our lives. Ask yourself today, "What can I accomplish for myself, for others, and for the Lord, if I would only maintain a spirit of humility and a childlike dependence upon God?"

PRAYER

Lord, I ask that You do such a mighty work in my heart now, that I will automatically turn to You for help with all of my daily tasks, endeavors, and intentions. Remind me that even if I've done a task a hundred times, You still long for me to commit it to You and to seek Your involvement. Thank You for helping me to develop and maintain a spirit of humility that will open the door to Your greatest blessings!

Blessed To Impress

*How great is your goodness, which you have stored up
for those who fear you, which you bestow in the
sight of men on those who take refuge in you.*

PSALM 31:19

After I dedicated my children to the Lord about seven years ago, my son John began taking an interest in art. He had never demonstrated any real artistic talent as he was growing up, so it never occurred to me or my husband to encourage him to take art lessons. But by the time he was a junior in high school, he was showing some impressive artistic abilities. His art teacher encouraged him to enter the annual art show, and though he had some misgivings, John decided to submit some of his best work. I knew that if my son won first place in the show, it would really boost his confidence and self-esteem. Because he led his public high school's Bible club and wore Christian T-shirts almost every day, there were times when he was ridiculed and even threatened by other students. I knew that winning the art show, which drew a lot of attention at his school each year, would help John to win the respect of his teachers and fellow students. So I began praying earnestly for my son to win. He was competing with students who had taken art lessons since they were very young and who showed great promise as artists, so I prayed that God would give John favor in the sight of all the judges and everyone else involved in the contest. When my family and I got the news that John won first place in the art show, we were awestruck. But it wasn't until we went to school and saw all the art work he was competing against that we realized what a miracle the Lord had worked on our behalf. And as we had hoped, John won the respect and admiration of his teachers and fellow students as a result of his recognition.

Some Christians might have felt uncomfortable praying as I did for my son to win the art show. But I believe that it's completely scriptural to ask God to bless us in ways that cause us to stand out. Isaiah 61:9 says that "All who see [us] will acknowledge that [we] are a people the Lord has blessed." And Isaiah 66:14 TLB says, "All the world will see the good hand of God upon his people." Psalm 112:6 TLB promises that "God's constant care of [us] will make a deep impression on all who see it." All of these verses indicate that the Lord wants to bless us so radically that it will be evident to others. When my son's art work won first place, the respect he gained from others enhanced his witness as a Christian and as the leader of the school's Bible club. So John's win didn't only benefit him—it inspired others and glorified God. There's nothing wrong with asking God for favor and blessings if we do so with a right heart. Genesis 12:2 reveals that one of the main reasons God blesses us is so that we can be a blessing to others. It's difficult to be

LIVE ON PURPOSE TODAY

Are you ready to stand out for the Lord and let your light shine? Consider three areas of your life today where you possess special talent and ask God to bless them. Trust Him for favor and promotion upon those talents so that all the world will recognize you walk with the Lord.

a blessing to others when you're not blessed yourself! But be prepared, because the devil is not going to stand idly by while you strive to stand out for God's glory. He's going to put people in your path who will become offended by your blessings so that you'll feel so guilty and condemned that you'll be tempted to apologize for them. But don't do it. Keep praying for the Lord's favor and blessings, knowing that they will bring Him the honor that He deserves. May this promise from God be planted deep in your heart today: "Your goodness is so great! You have stored up great blessings for those who honor You. You have done so much for those who come to You for protection, blessing them before the watching world"! (Ps. 31:19 NLT).

PRAYER

Lord, please give me an understanding of how and why it's Your desire to bless me and my loved ones. Help me to always pray for Your blessings for the right reasons, rather than out of pride or selfishness. Teach me how to share my blessings cheerfully and generously. Thank You that my blessings will impress others and glorify You!

Prayer That Gets Results

And so it is with prayer—keep on asking and you will keep on getting; keep on looking and you will keep on finding; knock and the door will be opened. Everyone who asks, receives; all who seek, find; and the door is opened to everyone who knocks.

LUKE 11:9,10 TLB

I used to wonder why Jesus used so many parables to get His point across. I have a better understanding of that now because of how many times God has used things in my own life to teach me. He taught me a wonderful lesson about prayer, using my bathtub as an illustration. At one point I couldn't get it clean, no matter how strong a cleaner I used on it. Finally, I gave up and resorted to using a simple household cleaner, just to reassure myself that at least the tub was sanitary. I faithfully maintained that tub a little each day, and I was amazed when I realized some weeks later that the tub sparkled! God showed me that it's often the same way with prayer. If I faithfully prayed each day for the things He put on my heart—for myself and others—He would work wonders as a result. He assured me that I didn't have to get ten people to agree in prayer with me, and I didn't need to have a famous evangelist pray for me. While those things can be good, I believe that most of the time the only way we can receive the answers to our prayers is by praying and standing in faith day after day. This is why, when Jesus was teaching on prayer in the above verses, He said we should keep on asking, seeking, and knocking.

Right before Jesus speaks these verses, He tells the parable of the persistent man who knocks on his friend's door at midnight to

LIVE ON PURPOSE

Pick one single thing today that you want to believe God for, and don't lose sight of it. Find Scriptures that promise your answer and go to the Father in prayer. With day in and day out faithfulness, thank God for the answer. And before long, victory will be yours.

appeal to him for bread. The Master concludes the story by saying, "But I'll tell you this—though he won't do it as a friend, if you keep knocking long enough, he will get up and give you everything you want—just because of your persistence. And so it is with prayer…" (Luke 11:8,9 TLB). It's then that He instructs us to ask, seek, and knock. This kind of prayer speaks of urgency and desperation. It's not a fainthearted, hit-or-miss kind of prayer. It's not for quitters or for halfhearted believers. One reason we don't see God's people enjoying more answered prayer is because we have a tendency to give up before we receive the answer. Through the grace of God, our prayers can bring salvation to the lost, healing to the sick, and deliverance to the oppressed. But only if we persist. What happens when we don't keep asking, seeking, or knocking? We don't receive, we don't find, and the door isn't opened. Just like my tub suffers when I neglect it, our prayer life will suffer from neglect, too. Don't be a quitter. Persist in prayer and receive all the blessings God has in store for you and the ones you love!

PRAYER

Lord, teach me how to ask, seek, and knock the way You want me to. Increase my faith daily so that I'll pray and stand in faith for the people and things You put on my heart. Make me patient and persistent so that I won't quit and give up before the answer comes. Thank You for all the answered prayer I'll reap as a result!

Extra Goodies

A faithful man will abound with blessings.

PROVERBS 28:20 NKJV

When my son John told me that the folks in his office were planning to have a Christmas party, I offered to bake my cheesecake squares and chocolate chip cookie bars, knowing they had been a big hit with this group in the past. As I was preparing the goodies for travel, John asked me to make two extra containers for his friends, Mark and Mike. When I told my son that it didn't seem right to give extra goodies to just two of his coworkers, he explained that it was perfectly okay because of his special relationship with them. As I prepared the extra treats, I thought about how this scenario might relate to how God distributes His blessings. While it's true that the Lord bestows a certain amount of blessings on everyone, it's also true that He blesses some people with "extra goodies." It's been said that God does not have "favorites," but that He does have "intimates." These are the people who have a personal relationship with the Lord and who seek Him daily, desiring to please and glorify Him with their lives. The Bible says, "Friendship with the Lord is reserved for those who fear Him. With them He shares the secrets of His covenant" (Ps. 25:14 NLT). Those who have a reverential respect for God, and who put their wholehearted trust in Him, will enjoy a unique relationship with Him. They will receive divine revelation when they need it most, and they will see the Lord fulfill His promises on their behalf. Most of all, God's presence will accompany them daily.

This experience also reminded me of the Savior's words in John 12:26: "My Father will honor the one who serves Me." When

LIVE ON PURPOSE TODAY

Find a pen and paper, and make note of how you can restructure your daily priorities to offer God more time. Begin by asking yourself what is most important in life. The answer to that question will make the rest easy.

I found out about the special relationship Mark and Mike had with my son, I was eager to bless them above and beyond the others in the group. How much more does the Father desire to shower with blessings those who honor His Son! If you have put your trust in Christ as your personal Savior and Lord, you should be receiving "extra goodies" from heaven daily. If you are not, you need to talk to the Lord about it. While some of His blessings are given simply because you have committed your life to Him, many are reserved for those who actively seek Him daily in prayer, praise, and the reading of His Word. Ask the Lord to show you how to restructure your priorities so that you can spend quality time alone with Him each day. Then be sure to maintain a lively expectation of His "bonus blessings" continually. This is not an attitude that says, "You owe me," to God. But it is a respectful expectation of God's faithfulness to His character and His Word. Lastly, make it a point to ask for "extra goodies" from the Lord. Do your part, knowing that God is sure to do His!

PRAYER

*Lord, show me how to have a personal, intimate relationship
with You, and help me to nurture it daily. Teach me how to
pray for and expect Your blessings in a way that pleases You.
Thank You that as You shower me with "extra goodies,"
I will be blessed and You will be glorified!*

The Dangers of Strife

*For where envying and strife is, there is
confusion and every evil work.*

JAMES 3:16 KJV

Several years ago I was driving my son to the public library to return some books he had borrowed for a project at school. I didn't like driving this route because it meant that we had to travel to the downtown area of a nearby city. I never felt comfortable having to deal with all the one-way streets. But I had prayed and stood on Psalm 91, which promises believers angelic protection, and I pushed my fears aside and depended on the Lord to watch over us. A few blocks before the library we got lost. Suddenly, I found myself yelling at my son and blaming him for not knowing which way we should go. A moment later my car collided with another, and what started out as a minor argument ended up in total disaster. No one was hurt, thank God, but both cars were damaged considerably. I must confess that the thing that bothered me most is that I had prayed for the Lord's protection right before the accident. I began to earnestly seek God about it, and He revealed to me that He allowed the accident to serve as a lesson about how destructive strife can be. When I got into strife with my son, I opened the door for Satan to come in and "steal, kill and destroy" (John 10:10). This shouldn't surprise us because the Bible indicates that we may forfeit angelic protection when we walk in disobedience. (Ps. 91:11 AMP; Ex. 23:20,21.) The verse above from James gives some insight into strife's destructive nature. The dictionary defines *strife* as "conflict, disagreement, discord, animosity, fighting, struggle, combat."[1] Looking at this long list of destructive behaviors, it's easy to understand why the Bible condemns strife.

Jesus said that the prayer of agreement has awesome power. (Matt. 18:19.) So we shouldn't be surprised when Satan works overtime to create division and dissension among believers. The devil knows that if he can disrupt the harmony of a family, church, or group, he can drastically reduce their prayer power. What's at the root of strife? Animosity is one cause. Proverbs 10:12 says, "Hatred stirs up strife." If we examine why we have a tendency to get into strife with a certain individual, we will often discover that we are harboring resentment or bitterness toward them. But if we make a quality decision to forgive and love that person, peace and healing will spring forth. Another cause of strife is pride. Proverbs 13:10 says, "Through insolence (pride) comes nothing but strife." The fruit of pride is always rotten, and when we choose to take a prideful attitude instead of one of humility, we are inviting trouble. One of the most destructive aspects about pride is that it can be so subtle that we don't even recognize it. When we find ourselves in conflict with someone, we should promptly seek God about it and ask Him, "Lord, if I'm harboring any resentment or pride in my heart, reveal it to me and help me to deal with it Your way." Praying a prayer like this with sincerity and remorse

LIVE ON PURPOSE TODAY

Go through your day looking to stamp out strife wherever it might raise its ugly head. Promise yourself that you will be quick to forgive, quick to repent, and the first in any situation to say, "I'm sorry."

will touch the heart of God and move Him to begin making the changes in us and our circumstances that need to be made. In 1 Corinthians 3:3 NASB, the apostle Paul writes, "For you are still fleshly. For since there is jealousy and strife among you, are you not fleshly?" Paul is saying here that believers who have a tendency to cause strife are worldly and spiritually immature. These people need to focus on cultivating a more intimate, meaningful relationship with God so they will demonstrate more Christlike behavior. The Lord calls us to "be imitators of God" and to "live a life of love" (Eph. 5:1,2). It's important for us to understand that strife needs to be taken seriously. If you are encountering strife in your family, church, or ministry, you need to confront it and deal with it swiftly and surely. Work hard at pursuing and maintaining peace, and know that when you do, you are engaging in powerful spiritual warfare that will bring a harvest of victory!

PRAYER

Lord, whenever I get into strife, convict me by Your Spirit and make me quick to repent. Remind me that Your Word says, "A troublemaker plants seeds of strife" (Prov. 16:28 NLT). Give me a desire to seek You daily through prayer, praise, and Bible study so that I'll become more like Jesus each day. Thank You for teaching me to be a peacemaker, instead of a troublemaker!

Getting Alone With God

"Yet the news about Him spread all the more, so that crowds of people came to hear Him, and to be healed of their sicknesses. But Jesus often withdrew to lonely places and prayed."

LUKE 5:15

Some time ago I saw a TV program about how focusing our concentration on something can affect our brainwaves. I was most fascinated by a demonstration by a marksman. As he initially pointed his gun at the target, his brainwaves showed little change. But as he took careful aim, tuning out all distractions around him and focusing intently on the target, his brainwave patterns were radically altered. This test revealed the precise moment when the marksman pulled the trigger, because it indicated the increased intensity of his focus and concentration, just before he fired his weapon.

This demonstration reminded me of how we can "take aim" with our prayers the same way. While it's true that we can pray anywhere, anytime, it's also true that there are times when we need to separate ourselves from the distractions of the world, so that we can focus intently on our communication with God, aiming our prayers with precision. This is one of the reasons why there is simply no substitute for spending time alone with God. Jesus demonstrated this principle perfectly. The Bible records numerous times when the Savior "went off to a solitary place, where He prayed" (Mark 1:35). If the Son of God needed to spend regular time alone with His heavenly Father, how much more do we need to? Jesus was a busy Man, and He had important work to accomplish. The verse we read at the beginning in Luke 5 tells us that crowds of people with pressing needs were constantly demanding His attention. Even so, we're told that "Jesus often withdrew to lonely places and prayed." The Savior knew how important it was for Him to regularly withdraw from the distractions and pressures of the world around Him, and to focus His attention solely on God. Just before He went to the Cross, when His anxiety and anguish were at their peak, Jesus withdrew to the Garden of Gethsemane to pour out His heart to God. As Christians, we have the same privilege. Jesus told His disciples, "When you pray, go away by yourself, shut the door behind you, and pray to your Father secretly. Then your Father, who knows all secrets, will reward you" (Matt. 6:6 NLT). When we make the effort to get alone with God and to prayerfully focus our attention solely on Him, He will reward us with untold blessings that we may not receive any other way. One of these blessings is divine revelation. Mark 4:33-34 says, "With many similar parables, Jesus spoke the word to them, as much as they could understand. But when He was alone with His disciples, He explained everything." This passage not only emphasizes how the Lord uses His Word to speak to us, but it also reveals how He takes special care to explain things more fully to those who spend time alone with Him.

It's been said that "God speaks to those who listen." God wants to speak to every one of His children, but He doesn't want to compete with the radio, TV, or anything else that steals our attention. The devil has seen to it that our lifestyle is embracing more and more noise. And the sad part is that we've become so accustomed to the noise and distractions around us, that we've almost forgotten how pleasant and soothing peace and quiet can be. Several years ago I began challenging myself to limit the amount of noise and distractions I come in contact with each day. I began to leave the radio off when I was driving my car, and I used this time to pray and fellowship with the Lord. I also began doing household chores in complete silence, using the time to meditate on Scripture and sing praises to God. Making these little changes in my life helped me to become more attuned to God's "still, small voice" and to grow closer to Him. Hearing an encouraging word from a friend, or in a sermon, can really make a difference in our lives. But nothing can impact us the way that hearing a direct word from God can. The Lord is able to speak words of wisdom and comfort like no one else can, and He longs to do exactly that. But we must do our part by making an effort to separate ourselves from the hustle and bustle of our daily lives, and to sit quietly in His presence. When we do, the Lord will not only speak to our hearts, but He will also refresh us and give us rest. The Bible tells us about a time when Jesus and His disciples were so busy that they didn't even have a chance to eat. The Savior told them, "Come with Me by yourselves to a quiet place and get some rest" (Mark 6:31,32). The Lord extends this same invitation to us every day. May we always choose to accept it, so that we may experience God's awesome presence, power, and peace in life-changing ways!

LIVE ON PURPOSE TODAY

Since the Lord is extending an invitation for you to come into His presence, don't keep Him waiting! Make an appointment with Him today—a time and a place when you will set aside the busyness of life and enjoy fellowship with your Father.

PRAYER

Lord, forgive me for the times I've failed to give You first place in my life. Do a new work in my heart, so that I will do whatever it takes to get alone with You for a while each day. Teach me how to tune out the noises and distractions around me, so that I can tune in to Your voice and aim my prayers with precision. Thank You, Lord, for leading me into a deeper and more rewarding relationship with You!

Testing Will Surely Come

{ *Testing will surely come.*

EZEKIEL 21:13 }

These days my husband's job situation is a source of a lot of tension and frustration for him. He's presently working under a man who by most people's standards would be considered totally unreasonable and unfair. Yesterday Joe and I were discussing the matter and wondering what God's purpose could possibly be in all this misery. When I suggested that it might be a test of some sort, Joe had to agree. I told him that his best bet would be to settle down and pass this test so that he wouldn't have to go through it again sometime in the future. I reminded him of how we moved out of our last home to escape our neighborhood problems, only to move into a new home where we encountered even more serious ones. He began to get the point.

It's only natural for us to want God to change our circumstances when they are causing us grief or pain. But the truth is that there are times when God will not change our circumstances until our circumstances change us. Even though the Lord may not be the One who brings adversity into our lives, He may still choose to use our difficulties to smooth the rough edges off of us so we can become more like Jesus. I believe it's right for us to pray for deliverance from our problems, but I think we should always ask God what He might be trying to teach us through them. I also think it's wise that when we pray for deliverance, we also pray that the Lord will help us to do our part in the process. The Bible says, "Testing will surely come" (Ezek. 21:13). The good news is that whenever we're tested and tried, God always has a reward in store for us if we pass the test. Often we'll experience severe hardship and adversity just before we receive a great promotion or blessing from the Lord. And we shouldn't be surprised that the enemy of our souls is behind our trouble, trying to keep us from making spiritual progress. We need to keep reminding ourselves that God has given us His Spirit to deal with and overcome difficult situations and people. My husband keeps saying that there's simply no way he can deal with his boss. But the truth is that God has already made a way. All that's necessary now is for my husband to line his will up with the Lord's so he can pass this test and move up to the next level. If Joe decides instead to run from his problems by quitting his present job, chances are that he'll like his new boss even less than his old one. If you are in a hard place right now, take comfort in the knowledge that the Lord will use your adversities to your advantage somehow. Set your mind to do God's will and declare with Job, "When He has tested me, I will come forth as gold"! (Job 23:10).

LIVE ON PURPOSE TODAY

Are you facing troubling situations that bear great resemblance to troubling situations of the past? If so, begin writing down changes you can make that will help you pass the test this time. With God's help you can make the grade!

PRAYER

Lord, please give me the discernment I need to recognize tests when they come my way. Help me to pass my tests the first time so that I won't have to go through them again. Remind me to spend time in Your presence daily so that You can impart to me the wisdom and strength I need to do Your will. Thank You that as I cooperate with Your Spirit, I will pass my tests and receive all the blessings You have in store for me!

The Proper Faith Response

> *Shadrach, Meshach and Abednego replied to the king,*
> *'O Nebuchadnezzar, we do not need to defend ourselves*
> *before you in this matter. If we are thrown into the blazing*
> *furnace, the God we serve is able to save us from it, and He*
> *will rescue us from your hand, O king. But even if He does*
> *not, we want you to know, O king, that we will not serve*
> *your gods or worship the image of gold you have set up.'*
>
> DANIEL 3:16-18

Last year one of my dearest relatives, my Aunt Trina, was stricken with cancer. She was a woman of faith, and when she received her doctor's grim diagnosis, she placed her trust firmly in God. My aunt's unshakable faith inspired me to ask the Lord for a complete recovery on her behalf. My loved ones and I sought prayer support from literally thousands of fellow believers. We were certain that God would work a miracle on my aunt's behalf. Nevertheless, her surgeries and treatments led to one complication after another, and though my aunt fought bravely to recover, she died a few months later. I was devastated, and for a while I felt numb. I still loved God and believed in Him, but my faith was shaken, and I was no longer sure if I could really depend on Him.

It was then that the Lord reminded me of an inspiring teaching I had heard some years earlier. A godly woman, whose husband was the pastor of a large church, told the story of how a little girl in their congregation had contracted a life-threatening illness. This woman was certain that God wanted to grant this child a miraculous healing, so she called for an all-night prayer vigil at her church. A multitude of faith-filled prayers went up to the Lord on behalf of this child, but a short time later she died. This pastor's wife cried out to the Lord in anguish, saying, "How can I ever feel like I can count on You again, after You've allowed this child to die like this?!" The Lord led her to the passage we read earlier from the Book of Daniel, and He told her that the faith response that these three Hebrew youths had in the midst of adversity was the same one He expected of her, even where this child's illness was concerned. It's a familiar Bible account. Shadrach, Meshach, and Abednego refuse to bow down to the king's golden idol, an offense that was punishable by death. Just before they are thrown into the fiery furnace, they declare that, not only is their God *able* to save them, but He *will* save them. But they make it clear that whether God chooses to rescue them or not, they will remain faithful to Him. As a result, they are rewarded with a miraculous rescue that has inspired believers throughout the ages.

LIVE ON PURPOSE TODAY

Make up your mind and shore up your heart with the determined choice that you will serve God every day in every way—in, through, and on your way out of adversity.

Through this inspiring Bible account, the Lord was telling this pastor's wife that He wanted her to continue to pray in faith for divine help and deliverance in times of trouble. But He also wanted her to make up her mind ahead of time that no matter what the outcome was, she would remain faithful to Him. Some years ago, when my oldest son, Joseph, was so bent on rebellion that my husband and I had to ask him to leave our home, I did two things: I prayed and trusted God to change my son's heart, so that we could be a whole and peaceful family again; and I decided with finality that even if the Lord never answered my prayers, I would still love Him and serve Him with all my heart. I believe that this is the kind of faith response that God often wants us to have in times of adversity. I'm happy to say that the Lord *did* eventually restore my family. But there have been many times when I've stood in faith for something and my prayers were not answered the way I had hoped. Even so, I continue to believe God for miracles every day, and I'm constantly amazed at how ready and willing the Lord is to give us the desires of our hearts.

The next time adversity is staring *you* in the face, I urge you to declare as Shadrach, Meshach, and Abednego did—"My God is able to save me, and He *will* rescue me!" But do it with a firm resolve that no matter what happens, you will love and serve the Lord with all your heart!

PRAYER

Lord, forgive me for the times I lost faith in You when my prayers weren't answered the way I expected. Teach me how to pray and stand in faith for You to work miracles on my behalf when I'm faced with adversity. Make me steadfast in my devotion to You, so that I will remain faithful to You, even when I don't get my way. Thank You that You are worthy of my trust, devotion, and praise!

Stubbornness Vs. Surrender

The Lord says, "I will guide you along the best pathway
for your life. I will advise you and watch over you.
Do not be like a senseless horse or mule that
needs a bit and bridle to keep it under control."

PSALM 32:8,9 NLT

A week before my son's wedding last month, my husband,
Joe, and I went shopping for shoes that would match my
dress. I had my heart set on wearing white shoes, even
though my friends and family told me that it was too late in the
year to wear them at an evening affair. I didn't care much for any of
the alternate colors they suggested, so I began combing the stores
for white shoes. To my dismay, my husband and I came up empty
after searching countless stores in our area. White dress shoes
were scarce, and when we did find a pair, they weren't available in
my size. I had been praying all this time, and I was baffled by the
fact that my pleas for the Lord's help were going unanswered. Out
of desperation, we checked a store that we would never have
checked otherwise. When we realized they didn't have any white
shoes for me, my heart sank. I felt defeated and weary. I told the
Lord that if He didn't show me what else to do, I was just going to
wear an old pair of white shoes I had at home. It was then that I
spotted a beautiful pair of sparkly silver dress shoes. I made a
quick, silent plea to God, and I asked the salesperson if they had
them in my size. She said that they had just gotten in a huge ship-
ment because so many people were wearing them to weddings. I
could have hugged her. I tried them on, and Joe and I both agreed
that they were perfect. The night of my son's wedding, people kept
coming up to me and telling me how much they loved my shoes,

asking me where I bought them and if they could take pictures of them. It was such an awesome experience that after the wedding, I left my new shoes out in my living room for days, just gazing at them and marveling at the goodness of God.

The thing that disturbed me most about this experience was that I had no idea I was out of God's will when I was shopping for white shoes. I sought the Lord about my endeavor, and I believed I had His approval. I didn't realize how stubborn I was acting when I had made up my mind to buy white shoes, and I expected the Lord to follow my plan. It wasn't until I searched in vain for what I wanted that I began to suspect that my plans and God's were not the same. After this experience, the Lord showed me the verses we just read from Psalm 32, which were confirmation of my willful behavior. These Scriptures assure us that God is eager to guide and advise us, but He expects our cooperation. He longs to give us His best, but He can't do that if we're fighting Him all the way. I've discovered over the years that when we're seeking the Lord and we're in His will, there's usually a "flow." That doesn't mean that we won't encounter some obstacles that are satanic in origin, but that overall, God's Spirit is leading us and working to bring our plans to pass. Numbers 22:32 NLT says, "I have come to block your way because you are stubbornly resisting me." This is an example of how God may choose to thwart our efforts if we are resisting His

LIVE ON PURPOSE TODAY

You've asked the Lord to remind you when you're stubborn. Now, take one more brave step. Find someone you're very close to, and ask him or her to honestly point out your stubborn ways to you, if there are any to be found.

will. At other times, the Lord may decide to let us go our own way so that suffering the consequences of our willfulness may help us come to our senses. In Psalm 81:11-12, He says, "But my people would not listen to me; Israel would not submit to me. So I gave them over to their stubborn hearts to follow their own devices." Sometimes the Lord will use others to correct us or give us godly wisdom. In these cases, it's for our own benefit that we heed what they say. Proverbs 29:1 NLT warns, "Whoever stubbornly refuses to accept criticism will suddenly be broken beyond repair." We need to realize that stubbornness is offensive to God, and He takes it very seriously. This is evident in many verses in the Bible, including 1 Samuel 15:23 NLT, which says, "Rebellion is as bad as the sin of witchcraft, and stubbornness is as bad as worshiping idols." The truth is that God wants to bless us even more than we want to be blessed. But we have to trust Him and follow Him, believing that He always wants what is best for us. In Isaiah 1:19, He makes this appeal: "If you are willing and obedient, you will eat the best from the land." And in Isaiah 48:17, He says, "I am the Lord your God, who teaches you what is best for you, who directs you in the way you should go." That day I was shoe shopping, God wasn't trying to withhold His blessings from me. He was trying to bless me above and beyond anything I could imagine. Only when I surrendered to His will was I able to receive His best. May David's prayers be ours today—"Keep Your servant from willful sins. Make me willing to obey You" (Ps. 19:13; Ps. 51:12 NLT).

PRAYER

Lord, when I am tempted to resist Your will and go my own way, remind me that Your Word says, "The stubborn are headed for serious trouble" (Prov. 28:14 NLT). On the basis of Your promise, I ask that You heal me of my willful ways, and guide and comfort me. (Isa. 57:18 AMP.) Thank You that as I am willing and obedient, the best of Your blessings will be mine!

Waiting for God's Best

Yet the Lord longs to be gracious to you;
he rises to show you compassion.
For the Lord is a God of justice.
Blessed are all who wait for him!

ISAIAH 30:18

No one likes to wait. Especially these days. Our society is used to having what we want, when we want it. But this is not God's way. The Bible is filled with stories and verses about the value of waiting on God. In God's kingdom, timing is everything. If you look at the lives of most of the great men and women of the Bible, you see that they had to endure long periods of waiting before their God-given purpose was fulfilled. Abraham had to wait many years before his promised son was born. Moses was 80 years old before God called him to lead the Israelites out of Egypt. Joseph endured long years of injustice before Pharaoh put him in charge of all Egypt. David suffered many years of persecution at the hands of Saul before he became king. And the list goes on. God used periods of waiting to prepare these people for the extraordinary blessings He had in store for them.

Sometimes it seems that God has put us on a shelf. It can be bewildering, frustrating, and depressing. We have a hard time trying to imagine any good coming out of it. One of the hardest parts is having to face all of the well-meaning people who keep saying, "What are you going to do?" You feel like you've done all that you can do. But that doesn't stop you from trying to come up with something. Then it occurs to you that maybe there's a way you can "help God." And you try to think of ways to "make something happen." Listen. If you really want to help God—trust Him. When He makes you wait, there's a good reason for it. The fact is, there are some blessings we are never going to receive

LIVE ON PURPOSE TODAY

As you read these words, were you prompted to slow down and become more patient in any area of life? If so, acknowledge that the Holy Spirit is speaking to you and respond aloud by saying, "Lord, I got the message. I will wait more patiently." That's sometimes all He's waiting on.

unless we wait for them. Yes, these times of waiting are uncomfortable for us. Sometimes they're downright painful. But if we try to make our own way instead of waiting on God, we will miss out on God's best for us. Let me encourage you today with some words from a man who had to do a lot of waiting in his life, but who was blessed beyond belief. In Psalm 27:14, David says, "Wait for the Lord; be strong and take heart, and wait for the Lord"!

PRAYER

Lord, You know how hard waiting is for me. Please give me the patience I need to wait for Your perfect timing in everything. Help me not to settle for second best. When I'm tempted to "make something happen," speak to my heart and remind me what my impatience can cost me. Help me to not only wait, but to do so with a good attitude. Thank You for all the blessings You have in store for me!

Faithful in Little Things

He who is faithful in a very little thing is faithful also in much.

LUKE 16:10 NASB

Unless you are faithful in small matters,
you won't be faithful in large ones.

LUKE 16:10 NLT

When my son Joseph was a junior in high school, he felt led to attend the "See You at the Pole" event for the first time. It was his heart's desire to join fellow Christian students and teachers who gathered around their school flagpole to pray and praise the Lord. But when the actual morning arrived, Joseph was having second thoughts about attending because he was so gripped by fear that he felt sick to his stomach. After we sought God in prayer, Joseph "set his face like flint" and took his place next to all the other believers gathered at his school in the Lord's name. My son met a lot of wonderful new Christian friends that day, and they discussed the possibility of starting a Bible club and holding weekly meetings on campus for Bible study and prayer. The Lord gave me a burden to pray for this club to become a reality, even though there had never been a successful one in the history of the school. Weeks turned into months without any sign of a club forming, but I persevered in prayer. Then Joseph shared with me how he felt that God was calling him to approach the school authorities about starting weekly meetings. As he began the process of securing permission to launch a Bible club on campus, the Lord opened one door after another and our dream became a reality. Under Joseph's leadership and the subsequent leadership of my younger son, John, this club touched and changed the lives of a multitude of students from our community and many others.

When I was praying for a high school Bible club, it never occurred to me that the Lord would use my own son to start it. Many of the other Christian students had been believers a lot longer than my son, and in many ways, he lacked their spiritual maturity. Nevertheless, God chose Joseph and used him in awesome ways for His glory. I have no doubts that Joseph's attendance at the "See You at the Pole" event that day had everything to do with the Lord choosing him to launch and lead the club. And I also believe that my faithfulness in prayer for the club was linked to God's choosing my own son to start it. In addition, the Lord blessed me with some of the most exciting and rewarding years of my life by making me the "Club Mom." As my family and I have walked with God over the years, He has taught us how one small act of obedience on our part can lead to major blessings. Many people are waiting for a "big event" in order to obey God. What they fail to realize is that if they don't obey Him in small matters, their "big event" may never come. Jesus said, "Unless you are faithful in small matters, you won't be

LIVE ON PURPOSE TODAY

Surely as you read these words, little things God is asking of you began to pop into your mind. Make note of them with paper and pen, and then endeavor to demonstrate faithfulness to the Lord by checking off as many as possible before the sun goes down.

faithful in large ones" (Luke 16:10 NLT). Make no mistake—before the Lord will use us to make a difference in this world, we will be tested. We will have to prove to God that He can count on us to obey Him in seemingly insignificant matters, simply because He's the One doing the talking. The truth is that no job that He assigns us is insignificant in His sight. When the Lord leads us "just" to pray for someone or about something, we are partnering with Him just as much as when we're performing a task that brings us considerable recognition. You can bet that when God gives us a seemingly small matter to attend to, Satan will try to convince us that how we respond won't make any difference. He will try to get us to take our obedience casually. This is just one of the many tactics the enemy uses to try to keep us from fulfilling our God-given purpose. I encourage you to begin praying today that the Lord will make you sensitive and obedient to His voice, even in the smallest of matters. Rest assured that heartfelt prayers like these will open the door for God to fill your life with more purpose and meaning than you ever dreamed possible!

PRAYER

Lord, give me a new awareness of how important it is for me to obey You even in the smallest of matters. Make me sensitive and obedient to Your voice, and give me discernment to recognize the voice of the enemy. Don't let me miss out on Your perfect plans for my life. Thank You for making me faithful in little things so that I can be faithful also in much!

Our Rightful Source

This is what the Lord says: "Cursed is the one who
trusts in man, who depends on flesh for his strength
and whose heart turns away from the Lord....
But blessed is the man who trusts in the Lord, whose
confidence is in him. He will be like a tree planted
by the water that sends out its roots by the stream...."

JEREMIAH 17:5,7,8

I like the way God doesn't mince words. He makes it abundantly clear that He wants us to put our trust in Him and not man. He goes so far as to say that those who put their trust in people will be cursed. Isaiah 2:22 says, "Stop trusting in man, who has but a breath in his nostrils. Of what account is he?" I especially like the way David puts it in Psalm 60:11: "Give us aid against the enemy, for the help of man is worthless." And for those of us who are tempted to put our trust in leaders, Psalm 146:3 says, "Do not put your trust in princes, in mortal men who cannot save." But the verses above reassure us that those who put their trust in God will not have to fear or worry even in a year of drought, because they will always be fresh and fruitful!

A job can be a good thing, but God doesn't want us making it our source. If we do, when we lose it, we will have no means of support. On the other hand, if we make God our provider, even if we are jobless for a time, our needs will still be met. Doctors can definitely be a blessing. But if we rely only on their limited wisdom and leave God out of the picture, it could cost us our

LIVE ON PURPOSE

This would be a good opportunity to count your blessings literally one by one. What better way is there to properly recognize your source? As a testimony to God's goodness, begin to list on paper the ways He's blessed you the most, and then keep that list nearby to encourage yourself in times of trouble.

health—maybe even our lives. Spouses and parents can be wonderful gifts, but depending on them for all our needs can be disastrous if they're ever taken from us. The good news is that God is willing and able to be all that we need in this life. If you are looking for stability and security in this ever-changing world, make our unchangeable God the source of all your needs. Then you can exclaim with the psalmist, "O Lord Almighty, blessed is the man who trusts in you"! (Ps. 84:12).

PRAYER

Lord, forgive me for the times I put my trust in man, rather than in You. Help me to look to You for all my needs, including all my physical, emotional, and spiritual needs. Help me to realize that when I make You my source, my resources are boundless. Thank You that no matter what happens, I will always be blessed and fruitful!

The High Cost of Unforgiveness

For if you forgive men when they sin against you, your heavenly Father will also forgive you. But if you do not forgive men their sins, your Father will not forgive your sins.

MATTHEW 6:14,15

These verses illustrate what is perhaps the best reason for our being forgiving people. Jesus makes it clear that if we don't forgive others, we aren't forgiven by God. How we treat others is a major factor in determining the quality of our relationship with God. Even our prayer life is affected when our attitudes toward others are not right. In Mark chapter 11, when Jesus is teaching about mountain-moving faith, He concludes by saying that if we hold anything against anyone, we must forgive them. If we want our prayers to have power, we cannot hold grudges or harbor bitterness. In Matthew 5:23-24, Jesus tells us that before we offer a gift to God, if we have a grievance against anyone, we need to be reconciled with them. Then God will accept our gift.

If you are holding a grudge against anyone right now, or if you are in strife with anyone, consider this. You could be opening a door for the enemy to come in and destroy your life, marriage, family, or friendships. In 2 Corinthians 2:10-11, Paul talks about forgiving the sinner after the church disciplines him. He says, "And what I have forgiven...I have forgiven in the sight of Christ for your sake, in order that Satan might not outwit us. For we are

LIVE ON PURPOSE TODAY

If you know deep inside that you're harboring resentment toward another, decide now to forgive. You might ask, "Can I really do this?" You cannot afford not to. Forgive the person whether you "feel" like it or not, and you will be free!

not unaware of his schemes." Paul reveals that by withholding forgiveness, we can give the devil an advantage over us. I decided long ago that harboring resentment just isn't worth it. My relationship with God and my prayers are too valuable to me. Maybe you feel you have a right to withhold forgiveness from someone. But if you belong to the Lord, you gave up your rights when you became a member of His family. Colossians 3:13 says, "Bear with each other and forgive whatever grievances you may have against one another. Forgive as the Lord forgave you." How can we refuse to forgive others when God has so graciously forgiven us? Today, the Savior is reaching out to you and asking, "Won't you do it for Me?"

PRAYER

Lord, forgive me for all the times I've harbored resentment toward others. Give me a heart like Yours so that I may be quick to forgive. When I'm tempted to hold anything against anyone, remind me how graciously You have forgiven me. Give me the grace and the wisdom to avoid conversations and situations that might lead to strife. Thank You that as I practice forgiveness, I will be blessed with a closer relationship with You!

The Positive Power of Saying "No"

Since Jesus went through everything you're going through and more, learn to think like him. Think of your sufferings as a weaning from that old sinful habit of always expecting to get your own way. Then you'll be able to live out your days free to pursue what God wants instead of being tyrannized by what you want.

1 PETER 4:1,2 MESSAGE

I recently read about a minister of the Gospel whose grateful congregation had sent him on a cruise. During his trip he made the discovery that indulging his appetite had let it get totally out of control. I believe that reading about this man's experience was God's way of confirming that I was on the right track with my new eating habits. After having tried some popular diets that allowed the dieter to eat small quantities of anything they wanted—and after achieving dismal results—the Lord began instructing me to say "no" to many of my own natural desires, and to say "yes" to wiser ones. I discovered that the more I resisted having my own way where my eating was concerned, the more control I gained over my appetite. This control enabled me to not only lose weight, but to keep it off, as well.

The verses above from The Message Bible were life-changing for me. They made me realize how doing what I feel like doing all the time allows my natural desires to bully me. The more I give in to myself, the harder it becomes to discipline myself to do the right thing. On the other hand, the more I resist my natural impulses to indulge myself, the more control and freedom I gain—which is what God wants for His children. For instance, often when I go shopping and get the impulse to buy something, I begin to feel a "tension" between my flesh and my spirit. My flesh may say, "You can't pass this up—it's on sale!" But my spirit will give me a "check" about it, warning me to resist the urge to buy it. Then I have to decide which I want to please more—my spirit or my flesh. Either way, I will have to endure some kind of suffering. If I say "no" to myself, my flesh will suffer. If I say "yes" to myself, my spirit will suffer. I've discovered that if I can't get out of a situation without suffering somehow, it's best if I suffer in my flesh, rather than in my spirit. That's the attitude Jesus had, and that's what the verses above are referring to. The Living Bible puts it this way: "Since Christ suffered and underwent pain, you must have the same attitude he did; you must be ready to suffer, too. For remember, when your body suffers, sin loses its power, and you won't be spending the rest of your life chasing after evil desires, but will be anxious to do the will of God" (1 Peter 4:1,2 TLB). Every time we choose to suffer in our flesh rather than have our own way, sin's hold over us diminishes and it becomes easier to obey God. Before we accepted Christ as our Savior, there was no way we could have escaped the enslavement of sin. But with the gift of salvation comes the gift of the Holy Spirit and the power to

LIVE ON PURPOSE TODAY

Where have you been saying "yes," when you should have been saying "no"? When you have the answer to that question, find Scriptures that strengthen your "no," and remain steadfast in their support.

live a godly life in a fleshly body and a sinful world. God doesn't give us His Spirit just so we can live like the rest of the world. He gives us supernatural power so that we can say "no" to sin and live the abundant life that Jesus died to give us. Can we quench the Spirit's power working in us? Absolutely. If we continually ignore the Holy Spirit's conviction and leading, our hearts can become hardened and it can become increasingly difficult to hear God's "still, small voice." First Peter 1:14 in The Message Bible says, "Don't lazily slip back into those old grooves of evil, doing just what you feel like doing. You didn't know any better then; you do now." The truth is, you don't have to give in to your sinful nature anymore when it makes demands on you. The Bible says that you've been given a new nature (2 Cor. 5:17), and if you'll live your life with an attitude of total dependence upon God, you can enjoy the freedom that's found in doing His will. Don't let anyone tell you that doing what you feel like doing all the time will make you happy. The fact is that it will make you miserable. If you really want to enjoy your life and receive all the blessings God has for you, begin today to give yourself lots of daily doses of "No"!

PRAYER

Lord, when I'm tempted to have my own way against Your will, remind me of how my indulgence could harm my health, my finances, or my relationship with You or others. Help me to live a disciplined lifestyle so I can receive Your best in every area of my life. Thank You for the control and freedom that saying "no" to myself will bring!

You Can't Please People

> I, even I, am He who comforts you and gives you all
> this joy. So what right have you to fear mere mortal
> men, who wither like the grass and disappear?
> And yet you have no fear of God, your Maker—you have
> forgotten Him, the one who spread the stars throughout the
> skies and made the earth. Will you be in constant dread
> of man's oppression, and fear their anger all day long?
>
> ISAIAH 51:12,13 TLB

I've lived long enough to have discovered a very important fact of life—you can't please people. One of the things I love most about serving God and living for Him is that I no longer have to live in fear of people's disapproval. All I have to do is concentrate on pleasing God, who never changes, and I'll succeed in life. It's a freedom that I appreciate and can't live without. I began experiencing this freedom for myself when I started studying the Bible and discovering what God says about trying to be a people pleaser. Proverbs 29:25 NLT says, "Fearing people is a dangerous trap, but to trust the Lord means safety." Trying to win the approval of people can lead to disappointment, frustration, and emptiness. But seeking God's approval brings peace, contentment, and fulfillment. Those who strive to please others are often unstable. You can't count on them, and neither can God. They are often easily intimidated, and they can be talked into or out of something, even though their own hearts condemn them for it. The Bible says, "Do not fear their intimidation, and do not be troubled" (1 Peter 3:14 NASB). Right before Jesus' departure, He leaves

His disciples His perfect peace and tells them, "Do not permit yourselves to be fearful and intimidated and cowardly and unsettled" (John 14:17 AMP). Trying to please people will rob us of our peace, and because of that, it can harm our mental, emotional, and physical health. On the other hand, "The fear of the Lord leads to life: Then one rests content, untouched by trouble" (Prov. 19:23).

The good news is that we can depend on God all the time. He tells us in His Word, "I the Lord do not change" (Mal. 3:6). And James tells us that our God "does not change like shifting shadows" (James 1:17). Can you imagine if people recorded their own laws? They would have to be altered continually to keep up with our tendency to change the rules as we go along. But God won't ever change, and neither will His Word. God wants to bless us and use us for His glory, but He can't do that if we're busy trying to please others, instead of seeking His perfect will for our lives each day. The Bible says, "All who are led by the Spirit of God are children of God" (Rom. 8:14 NLT). It's God's will for us to be Spirit-led, not people-led. Otherwise, God will not be able to count on us, and He will have to put us on a shelf instead of using us to make a real difference in this world. The apostle Paul was a great example of a God pleaser, and the Lord used Him mightily. In Galatians 1:10 NLT, Paul exclaims, "Obviously, I'm not trying to be a people pleaser! No, I'm trying to please God. If I

LIVE ON PURPOSE TODAY

See how quickly you can put into practice the words just preached to you! Actively seek God *today*, ask for His guidance *today*, and then yield to the promptings of His Spirit *today*.

were trying to please people, I would not be Christ's servant." If we want to be true servants of Christ, we're going to have to actively seek God daily, ask for His guidance, and then yield to the promptings of His Spirit. Sometimes what people want us to do and what God wants us to do will be the same, but many times they will conflict. It's up to us to choose whom we will obey. If you are in the habit of trying to please people, remember this—it can't be done. My prayer for you today is that in everything, you'll set your heart on pleasing God and discover for yourself the peace and freedom that only He can give!

PRAYER

Lord, help me to seek Your perfect will in everything each day. Teach me to be sensitive and obedient to the promptings of Your Spirit. Guard me from the fear of man, and grant me a holy fear and reverence for You. Thank You for the peace, joy, and freedom I'll enjoy as a result!

Faith Doesn't Need
the "Big Picture"

*By faith, Abraham, when called to a place he would
later receive as his inheritance, obeyed and went,
even though he did not know where he was going.*

HEBREWS 11:8

This verse is one of many in the "Faith Hall of Fame" in
Hebrews chapter 11. Here, Abraham is honored because,
when God commanded him to leave his country and family
behind to go to a land the Lord "would show him" (Gen. 12:1), he
"obeyed and went." The Scripture adds, "…even though he did not
know where he was going." I can almost see Abraham gathering
all his belongings, saying good-bye to his relatives and friends, and
then heading off in the direction God pointed him in. That's
amazing enough, but can you imagine the exchange every time he
met someone on the way and they asked him, "So, where are you
headed, Abraham?" "Gee, I don't know. God just told me to leave
everything behind and head off in this direction." More than once,
I'm sure he heard, "You're a fool, Abraham!"

Maybe God is telling you today to set off in a new direction.
To leave your comfort zone behind. To head out into the unknown.
Perhaps the Lord is leading you a certain way, but He hasn't given
you any clue what's up ahead. God sees the "big picture," but
usually He only reveals to us a small piece of the puzzle at a time.
If He showed us more, we might run the other way out of fear. Or
we might feel like we could find our own way without Him.

LIVE ON PURPOSE TODAY

As you pray the prayer below, the Holy Spirit may quicken at least a few steps to your heart. Take a moment to write them down and purpose to act on them immediately.

Considering the outcome of his extraordinary life, you can bet that Abraham never regretted his decision to follow God. You won't regret it, either!

PRAYER

Lord, I ask Your forgiveness for the times I've failed to follow Your leading because of fear or stubbornness. Give me the courage and willingness I need to be sensitive to Your leading and to obey Your every command. If it's not Your will to show me the "big picture" right now, then show me enough to encourage me to take the first steps toward doing Your will. Thank You for the blessings that are up ahead for me!

You Have a Job To Do!

*For we are God's workmanship, created in Christ Jesus to
do good works, which God prepared in advance for us to do.*

ISAIAH 30:18

I f you have received salvation through faith in Christ, then this
verse applies to you and you need never again wonder if you
were created for a purpose. You are God's masterpiece, re-
created in Christ, to do good deeds and accomplish great things
for God's glory. These acts and achievements were prepared by
God in advance, before you were even born. You have a God-given
purpose. If anyone tells you otherwise, they are dead wrong. Satan
himself will try to convince you that you have no real purpose in
life. He may even use other people to do it. But if you fall for that
lie, you will live a meaningless, purposeless life. But you don't
have to! Jeremiah 29:11 says, "For I know the plans I have for
you," declares the Lord, "plans to prosper you and not to harm
you, plans to give you hope and a future."

When Jesus told the Parable of the Talents, He was letting
us know that each of us has a special purpose in life, and God
expects us to cooperate with Him so that it is fulfilled. All three
servants in the parable are given various talents, which represent
the individual's gifts and resources. The servants who put their
gifts to good use and were productive were rewarded by the
master. They were given more resources and greater responsibility.
But one of the servants was so fearful and self-centered that he
buried his talent and was totally unfruitful for the master. Jesus

LIVE ON PURPOSE TODAY

Take a moment to write down five things that you're very good at. Then keep that list close at hand—perhaps in the front of your Bible. Review it frequently and ask the Lord to show you how to use your talents for Him.

calls him a "worthless servant." If you are a child of God, He has blessed you with special gifts that He expects you to use for His glory. If you don't know what they are, ask Him to reveal them to you. Ephesians 5:15 AMP says that we should "live purposefully" and make the most of our time. You have a job to do! There may be people in this world right now who will never receive the gift of salvation unless you take your place in the body of Christ. It's my heartfelt prayer that you will make a decision today to cooperate with God's plan for your life and align your will with His. If you do, God's promise in Psalm 138:8 belongs to you—"The Lord will fulfill his purpose for me"!

PRAYER

Lord, today I commit to You all that I am and all that I have, and I ask that You fulfill Your purpose for my life. Show me what my gifts are and help me to use them for Your glory. Use me to lead others to You. The next time I doubt that my life has a special purpose, remind me of the truth. Thank You that You will fulfill Your purpose for me and that You will be glorified!

When Trouble Strikes

I will call to You whenever trouble strikes, and You will help me.

PSALM 86:7 TLB

For most of my life I had a mindset that almost expected trouble. I was raised as a Christian, and I was brought up hearing the Savior's words—"In this world, you will have trouble" (John 16:33). So it seemed natural to me that I should expect—and even count on—having problems throughout my life. As a result, when adversity struck me or my loved ones, my prayers for help were often timid and halfhearted. It wasn't until I was married and had teenaged children that I got serious about my relationship with God and began studying His Word. I was delighted to discover that the Bible was filled with godly men and women who boldly called upon the Lord in their times of trouble and were often delivered in miraculous ways.

One such person was King David. When we study David's life and writings, we discover that when this man of God encountered trouble, he was quick to call upon his divine Deliverer. David didn't just pray for relief or help—he prayed for victory. He didn't hesitate to pour out his heart to God, or to let the Lord know exactly what he was feeling. And he was humble enough to admit his need for God and his dependence upon Him. David wrote, "In the day of my trouble I will call to You, for You will answer me" (Ps. 86:7). I believe that this attitude of David's was one of the secrets of his enormous success.

Psalm 34 is one of the most quoted and beloved psalms in the Bible. In it, David mentions the delivering power of God three times. He says, "A righteous man may have many troubles, but the Lord delivers him from them all" (v. 19). David is not in denial. He freely admits that God's people are not exempt from problems. But he chooses to focus on God's ability and willingness to save and deliver. In verses 6 and 17 of this psalm, David reveals that God's entire rescue operation is put into action as a result of prayer. He writes, "The righteous cry out, and the Lord hears them; He delivers them from all their troubles" (Ps. 34:17).

It's true that Jesus said, "In this world, you will have trouble." But it's also true that He went on to say, "But take heart! I have overcome the world" (John 16:33). The Savior was not trying to discourage us with these words. He was trying to encourage our hearts and give us hope. He was telling us that even though we'll go through some hard times, they won't be able to defeat us, if we'll live our daily lives trusting in Him and depending on Him for guidance and strength. And even though there will be problems in our

LIVE ON PURPOSE TODAY

Select one of the Scriptures shared above and memorize it so that you can commit it to heart and mind. You'll find in the day of trouble it will rise up to help you!

lives that are simply unavoidable no matter what we do, there will be some that we can escape by making right choices. Proverbs 19:23 says, "The fear of the Lord leads to life: Then one rests content, untouched by trouble." This is God's assurance that by trusting and obeying Him, we can minimize the amount of trouble that we'll encounter in our daily lives. The psalmist wrote, "Blessed is the man You discipline, O Lord, the man You teach from Your law; You grant him relief from trouble, till a pit is dug for the wicked" (Ps. 95:12,13). Those believers who devote themselves to the Word of God—studying it and doing it—will be able to avoid many of the pitfalls that the enemy puts in their path. I know from experience that ignorance of God's Word can be costly and painful. Prayerlessness can be costly, too. We will encounter more trouble than we need to, if we fail to pray regularly for protection from it. Jabez prayed, "Keep me from all trouble and pain!" (1 Chron. 4:10 NLT). We know that God was pleased with his prayer, because Scripture says, "And God granted his request."

James wrote, "Is any one of you in trouble? He should pray" (James 5:13). Notice that he didn't say we should whine, complain, or get angry. He didn't say we should just accept our lot and be grateful that things aren't any worse. He said we should *pray*. This is a common theme throughout the Bible, and it's one we should take seriously and apply to our own lives. It's my heartfelt prayer that this precious invitation and promise from God would inspire and challenge you today: "Call upon Me in the day of trouble; I will deliver you and you will honor Me" (Ps. 50:15).

PRAYER

Lord, when trouble strikes, teach me to pray for deliverance with confidence and boldness. Help me to devote myself to You and Your Word so that I can avoid as many problems as possible. Thank You, Lord, that You will be with me in trouble as I call upon You; You will deliver me and honor Me, according to Your Word! (Ps. 91:15.)

The Price of Peace Is Prayer

Do not be anxious about anything, but in everything, by prayer and petition, with thanksgiving, present your requests to God. And the peace of God, which transcends all understanding, will guard your hearts and your minds in Christ Jesus.

PHILIPPIANS 4:6,7

These verses were the ones that convinced me that God really does want us to pray about everything. Here, Paul tells us that there is nothing in life that we should worry about. Then he says that, instead, we should pray about everything. When I first read these verses, I thought for sure there must be exceptions to the rule. Surely God has better things to do than to listen to my every little complaint or concern. Wrong. Look at it this way—whatever we don't pray about, we're going to worry about, right? And the point God is trying to make here is that He doesn't want us worrying about anything. That means that there's nothing that's too trivial to bring to God's attention in prayer.

Years ago I was told by well-meaning people that I was not to bother God with the little details of life. I have seen many precious people struggle with burdens that God is willing to lighten for them, all because they were under the impression that He's too busy or disinterested in their minor affairs. Now, when I tell you that I pray about everything, you can believe I mean everything. I don't wait until my little problems become big problems. I present them to God right away, and even when He doesn't answer my prayers the way I expect Him to, He always does something to ease the strain. Don't buy into that misconception that says God is not interested in every little detail of your life. Start today to pray about anything and everything that concerns you, and then enjoy the peace and satisfaction that settle over you when you do!

LIVE ON PURPOSE TODAY

What problems and frustrations did you carry yesterday that you could have turned over to the Lord? Make note of them so that today you can walk carefree!

PRAYER

Lord, I'm sorry for all the times I carried burdens I didn't have to, all because I neglected to bring them to You in prayer. Open my eyes and my heart, and help me to see how much You love me and how much You care about every little concern of mine. Whenever I am tempted to shoulder my burdens alone, please remind me to turn to You in prayer, and then surround me with Your perfect, healing peace.

You Will Know Them by Their Fruit

When you follow the desires of your sinful nature, your lives will produce these evil results: sexual immorality, impure thoughts, eagerness for lustful pleasure, idolatry, participation in demonic activities, hostility, quarreling, jealousy, outbursts of anger, selfish ambition, divisions, the feeling that everyone is wrong except those in your own little group, envy, drunkenness, wild parties, and other kinds of sin. Let me tell you again, as I have before, that anyone living that sort of life will not inherit the Kingdom of God. But when the Holy Spirit controls our lives, He will produce this kind of fruit in us: love, joy, peace, patience, kindness, goodness, faithfulness, gentleness, and self-control.

GALATIANS 5:19-23 NLT

I recently heard from a young woman who was bitterly disappointed in a young man she had allowed herself to get close to. She was well acquainted with God's commands in Scripture that tell us: "Do not be yoked together with unbelievers.... What does a believer have in common with an unbeliever? 'Therefore, come out from them and be separate, says the Lord'" (2 Cor. 6:14,15,17). And she was careful to make sure that her closest companions were Christians. But because she was so focused on this man's profession of faith, she failed to give serious attention to his un-Christlike behavior, and the relationship left her deeply hurt and disappointed.

As I prayed for this young woman and thought about her situation, the Lord impressed upon me a simple truth: A believer who acts like an unbeliever can do us just as much harm as someone who actually is an unbeliever. That's why the Scriptures command us to avoid close relationships with carnal (worldly) Christians. The apostle Paul wrote, "You are not to associate with anyone who claims to be a Christian yet indulges in sexual sin, or is greedy, or worships idols, or is abusive, or a drunkard, or a swindler. Don't even eat with such people" (1 Cor. 5:11 NLT). These sound like harsh guidelines for God's people, but they are necessary to prevent us from having a false sense of security around other Christians. I've seen many believers let their guard down around people they should have been more wary about, simply because these folks professed to be followers of Christ. Sadly, this casual attitude left these believers wide open to deception and destruction. Jesus said, "I am sending you out as sheep among wolves. Be as wary as snakes and harmless as doves" (Matt. 10:16 NLT). The Lord wants us to find the perfect balance between having suspicious minds and being gullible. He expects us to use godly discernment in all of our dealings with others. We can do that by being sensitive to the leading of the Holy Spirit, and by having a working knowledge of God's Word.

Jesus said, "By their fruit you will recognize them" (Matt. 7:16). The Savior knew that others would try to deceive us, and that's why He warned us to put people to the test by examining their actions. He told us not to just pay attention to their words, but to look at how they

LIVE ON PURPOSE TODAY

Take a moment to examine the spiritual fruit of your closest friends—to make sure they should remain your closest friends. Do you believe that God is pleased to observe love, joy, peace, patience, kindness, goodness, faithfulness, gentleness, and self-control in them?

live. He said, "Beware of false prophets who come disguised as
harmless sheep, but are really wolves that will tear you apart. You
can detect them by the way they act, just as you can identify a tree
by its fruit" (Matt. 7:15,16 NLT). Though the Lord was referring to
false prophets here, the principle is the same for others who would
attempt to mislead God's people. Jesus goes on to say, "Not all
people who sound religious are really godly. They may refer to Me
as 'Lord,' but they still won't enter the Kingdom of Heaven. The
decisive issue is whether they obey My Father in heaven" (Matt.
7:21 NLT). If the young woman who wrote me had given more
attention to this man's actions and less to his words, she might
have avoided being misled. But either because of ignorance or willfulness, she ignored the warning signs.

When we're faced with the possibility of forming a new relationship with someone, we shouldn't just ask ourselves, "Are they a
Christian?" But the real question should be, "Would this relationship
please and glorify God, and is it His will for me?" Scripture says,
"Above all else, guard your affections. For they influence everything
else in your life" (Prov. 4:23 TLB). The kind of relationships we make
and maintain will affect every aspect of our lives, either positively or
negatively. The choice is ours, and we should choose wisely.

PRAYER

*Lord, teach me how to devote myself to prayer and the study of
Your Word, so that I may develop the spiritual discernment I need to
avoid the relationships that are out of Your will for me. When I'm
inclined to get close to someone, remind me to examine their "fruit"
and to look for the characteristics that Your Word says believers
should exhibit: "love, joy, peace, patience, kindness, goodness,
faithfulness, gentleness, and self-control" (Gal. 5:22,23). Thank You
that as I seek to please and glorify You with my relationships,
You will bless me with godly, faithful, and loving companions!*

The Recipe for Success

Commit everything you do to the Lord.
Trust him, and he will help you.

PSALM 37:5 NLT

The Bible contains many promises related to the tasks we perform. The verse above is one of my favorites to pray and stand on whenever I have a job to do. Another one is Proverbs 16:3: "Commit your work to the Lord, and then your plans will succeed." God is eager to bless the work of our hands, and He wants us to succeed in all we do. Notice, though, that He wants us to first entrust our tasks to Him. God wants to be invited into every area of our daily lives, but He is a gentleman. He will not force His help on us. That's not His style. There's a certain amount of humility involved in our asking God for help, and often it's our pride that keeps us from asking. Other times it's the belief that it's not a big enough job to seek God's help with, or it's one that we've performed countless times before. I'm familiar with that way of thinking because I used to think that way myself. Now, no matter how small or insignificant my tasks seem, I ask God for His help, and I believe it pleases Him greatly. How do I know? Because overall, my work goes more smoothly, the results are better, and I experience more joy and satisfaction.

Next time you start to fix your hair or apply your makeup, ask for the Lord's help. When you're doing the laundry, mowing the lawn, or working on your car, invite God to help you. Commit all your child care and parenting duties to Him. Don't try to raise

LIVE ON PURPOSE TODAY

Purpose to seek God's help in every activity of the day. What one thing immediately comes to mind that you can commit to the Lord right now? As soon as you commit to Him, you've already begun following God's recipe for success!

kids these days without the divine assistance that God offers you. Don't try to drive without Him. Take the Lord along with you when you travel. And why would any child of God want to try to get through school without their heavenly Father's grace, power, and wisdom? If you're employed, bring God to your job each day, and ask Him to help you be the best employee your company's ever had. When you "commit everything you do to the Lord," you will have at your disposal the help of the Father, Son, and Holy Spirit, as well as a legion of angels, if necessary. Today, begin seeking God's help in all your endeavors, and you can bet "the Lord your God will make you successful in everything you do"! (Deut. 30:9 NLT).

PRAYER

Lord, I'm sorry that I've often left You out of my everyday activities. Help me to humble myself and ask You for help with everything I do. When I'm tempted to try to do things on my own, remind me of Your generous offer to help. Deliver me from an independent attitude, and help me to rely on You the way You desire. Thank You for the greater ease, joy, and success I'll find in all my tasks from now on!

Wait for the Harvest

Be patient, then, brothers, until the Lord's coming. See how the farmer waits for the land to yield its valuable crop and how patient he is for the autumn and spring rains. You, too, be patient and stand firm, because the Lord's coming is near.

JAMES 5:7,8

When my family became acquainted with Christian music years ago, we naturally wanted to share our enthusiasm with our friends and relatives. My boys, Joseph and John—who were teenagers at the time—seemed determined to get their teen cousins "turned on" to their new music. Whenever a gift-giving occasion came around, my boys would eagerly select and purchase music for their cousins that they hoped would be a blessing to them. This went on for a few years, until finally my sister had to tactfully let me know that buying Christian music for her daughters was a waste. My boys were heartbroken, but we talked about the situation and decided to leave the matter in God's hands. I sympathized with my sons because I, too, had a desire to see my own sister take an interest in music that glorified the Lord. My attempts to introduce her to my music were unsuccessful, so I eventually gave up trying, and I began praying for God to change her heart. A year or two later one of the ladies my sister worked with began sharing her love for Christian music with my sis, who began developing a love of her own for it. Now my sister delights in introducing me to new music that glorifies God, and we have a new common bond between us that has made our relationship even stronger.

This experience was a reminder to me that when we plant seeds of faith in the hearts of others, we usually have to endure a waiting period. If you're like me, you not only want to impact others' lives for God, but you want to see the fruit of your labor right away. But the Lord used the verses above to remind me that, like farmers planting their crops need to be patient and wait for their valuable harvest, we must patiently wait to see the results of our efforts for God's kingdom. While these verses actually relate to the Lord's Second Coming, I also see a principle at work here that helps me to understand how we must often wait upon God to reveal His presence and power in people's lives and circumstances. Through our prayers, words, and actions, we can plant seeds in the lives of others that will produce a harvest for their good and God's glory. But if we become too frustrated or anxious, we could literally dig up the seeds we've planted before they've had a chance to take root and bear fruit. There have been many times when I've become impatient with the spiritual progress of those around me—especially my closest loved ones—and out of anger and frustration, I've uprooted the seeds of faith I had tenderly planted in their hearts. In many cases, it took months—or even years—to undo the damage I had done in just a short time. I've had to learn the hard way that planting a harvest for God takes time, patience, and understanding. Now when I begin to get anxious and impatient with the spiritual growth of

LIVE ON PURPOSE TODAY

Ask the Lord to lead you to one person today in whose life you can plant a Gospel seed. Be willing to water the seed, nurture it with love, and give it ample time to grow.

others around me, I often think of my experience with my sister. It reminds me that even when it seems that my efforts are failing miserably, God could very well be working behind the scenes to make them fruitful somewhere down the line. I believe that as long as I am praying in faith and planting seeds according to God's leading, the Lord will keep working in that person's life somehow. I've seen God go to great lengths to put pressure on people and to surround them with believers, simply because I began praying for them and asking the Lord to change them. Now I take great comfort in knowing that even if I can't impact someone personally, God knows who can, and He will send the right person across their path as I pray for them in faith. I'm sharing all this with you today to encourage you not to give up on your efforts to influence others for God. Satan will try to convince you that all your prayers and seed planting are a waste of time and energy, but don't you believe it. Instead, put your hope in God, who's urging you today—"Be patient and stand firm, because the Lord's coming is near"!

PRAYER

Lord, when I'm tempted to become impatient with seeing the fruits of my labor for You, please remind me that my impatience can do more harm than good. Show me how to plant seeds of faith in people's lives, and to nurture them with prayer, godly behavior, and understanding. Thank You for the valuable harvests that will bless many and glorify You!

When All We Can
See Are Giants!

The land we passed through and explored is exceedingly good. If the Lord is pleased with us, he will lead us into that land, a land flowing with milk and honey, and will give it to us. Only do not rebel against the Lord. And do not be afraid of the people of the land, because we will swallow them up. Their protection is gone, but the Lord is with us. Do not be afraid of them.

NUMBERS 14:7-9

These are the words of Joshua and Caleb after returning from their exploration of the Promised Land, along with ten other "spies" sent out by Moses, their leader. God had promised the land of Canaan to the Israelites after He delivered them out of the hands of Pharaoh in Egypt. The Lord had told His people that the land He was giving them was lush and fertile—"a land flowing with milk and honey." When the twelve spies scouted out the land in advance, they discovered that "all the people there were of great size" (Num. 13:32), and as a result, ten of the spies brought back a "bad report." Only Joshua and Caleb declared that they were able to conquer the giants, because God was on their side. And because of their faith in God and His promises in the face of certain defeat, they were the only two spies that made it to the Promised Land.

You may have some giants looming in your life right now. They may be financial troubles or health problems, or problems with a parent, child, teacher, or boss. Maybe you've been struggling with your weight for years, and you don't see any way out. Whatever it is, remember Joshua and Caleb. When the other ten spies saw only giants, Joshua and Caleb saw God. There's a song that says, "Turn your eyes upon Jesus." If you'll do that today, God will see to it that you make it to the Promised Land!

LIVE ON PURPOSE TODAY

To help magnify God in your life and minimize your problems, go to God's Word and find Scriptures that promise you victory over the giants you face. Memorize at least one of those Scriptures and quote it throughout the day!

PRAYER

Lord, You know what I'm up against today. Sometimes my problems seem so big that all I can see is them and not You. Help me to take my eyes off the giants in my life and fix them on You. Cause me to realize how big a God You really are and how willing You are to face all my problems with me, if I'll let You. Thank You that with You beside me, the victory is mine!

The God of Comfort

> *What a wonderful God we have—he is the Father of our Lord*
> *Jesus Christ, the source of every mercy, and the one who so*
> *wonderfully comforts and strengthens us in our hardships and*
> *trials. And why does he do this? So that when others are*
> *troubled, needing our sympathy and encouragement, we can*
> *pass on to them this same help and comfort God has given us.*
>
> 2 CORINTHIANS 1:3,4 TLB

One day a few years ago I got a call from one of my sisters, saying that while my parents were flying home from vacation, my father died on the plane. My first reaction was disbelief. He had just called me a couple of days ago, telling me how he was looking forward to seeing me when he arrived home later that week. He was away for Father's Day and I had promised him a visit so we could celebrate. I already had his card and gift. The realization that I would never see my dad again threatened to overwhelm me, but I pushed it aside to think about my mother and what she must be going through now. She was all alone in a city far away from home, where she was surrounded by strangers in her time of need. One of the things that troubled me most at the time was how I would get through all the funeral services for my father. I was concerned about my mother and three sisters, and I wanted so much to be strong for them. I asked God for a miracle. I prayed that He would sustain me with His strength, comfort, and peace so that I could help and support my loved ones until my dad was laid to rest. God answered that prayer far above my expectations, and the example I set for my family was a powerful witness of His boundless love and mercy.

The verses above, written by the apostle Paul, have a very special meaning for me now. I have experienced firsthand how eager our God is to comfort us during difficult times, especially when we ask in faith. One reason He does this is so that we, in turn, can reach out to others in their times of trouble, offering them the same comfort we have received from the Lord. One of the things that impressed me most when I began studying the Bible was how many comfort-related verses there are. Jesus Himself said, "Blessed are those who mourn, for they will be comforted" (Matt. 5:4). Sometimes believers have the idea that when someone we love dies, especially if they were Christians, we shouldn't mourn or grieve for them. But that's not scriptural. God made grieving part of the healing process, and He gave us tears for a reason. Ever notice how good you feel after a good cry sometimes? The fact is that there are times when nothing will bring relief like a good cry can. On the other hand, God doesn't want us to sink into a pit of depression or despair. Nehemiah 8:10 NKJV says, "Do not sorrow, for the joy of the

LIVE ON PURPOSE TODAY

Ask the Lord to bring someone across your heart today in need of comfort. Then follow where Love leads you! Pick up the phone and speak words that encourage, or write a note that will inspire, or go and deliver hope.

Lord is your strength." Excessive sorrow can drain us of our strength and joy, and can eventually harm our mental and physical health. Each time I began feeling overwhelmed with sadness after my dad died, I claimed God's promise in Isaiah 53:4 NKJV: "Surely He has borne our griefs and carried our sorrows." Since Jesus took upon Himself all the misery we'll ever experience in this life, we can embrace the suffering that is part of God's healing process, and we can reject the suffering that would destroy our well-being. God's desire to comfort us is so great that He has given us His Holy Spirit, whom Jesus called the "Comforter," to abide in us continually. (John 14:16 KJV.) While there will be times when the Lord uses others to comfort us, we should never forget that our greatest source of comfort is only a prayer away. Another way that God offers us comfort is through His Word. Psalm 119:50 NLT says, "Your promise revives me; it comforts me in all my troubles." If you are in need of comfort today, may this promise from the Lord encourage your heart: "As a mother comforts her child, so will I comfort you" (Isa. 66:13).

PRAYER

Lord, when I am in need of comfort, help me to turn to You first. Teach me how to comfort others with the comfort You offer me. Remind me that You gave me tears for a reason, but don't let me drown in self-pity or despair. Thank You that through Christ, my comfort overflows! (2 Cor. 1:4.)

The Lord Will Provide

Abraham looked up and there in a thicket he saw a ram
caught by its horns. He went over and took the ram
and sacrificed it as a burnt offering instead of his son.
So Abraham called that place The Lord Will Provide.

GENESIS 22:13,14

In October of 2000, my son John wrecked his car in a five-car accident coming home from work. That's the bad news. The good news is that he wasn't injured, and neither was anyone else involved in the accident. After thanking God for keeping everyone safe, my husband, Joe, and I began discussing how we would deal with the unexpected vehicle shortage in our household. We prayed and asked the Lord what He would have us do. Then Joe remembered that he spoke to my sister earlier that day, and she mentioned that she had bought a new car and was donating her used van to charity. We prayed again, asking the Lord if He would have us approach my sister about buying the van from her. When we felt we had the Lord's approval, we called my sister and asked if she would agree to sell us her van. She sympathized with our sudden need for a vehicle, and she told us the van was ours if we wanted it. Two days later we drove our "new" van home, and my husband told everyone, "If that isn't God, I don't know what is!" I couldn't have said it better myself.

One of the things I love most about God is the way He goes ahead of us and provides for our needs before they even arise. John's accident didn't catch the Lord by surprise. He knew it was coming, and He went ahead of us and provided the van before we even knew we needed it. The morning of my son's accident, my sister called Joe at work to ask him a tax-related question (my husband being a part-time tax preparer). She was donating her old van and wanted to know how to handle the applicable tax deduction. We found out later that my sister had already mailed the ownership title for her van to the organization she was donating it to. But because she neglected to provide all the necessary documentation, the paperwork was sent back to her. She was just preparing to put it in the mail a second time when my husband called with his offer to buy the van. We've all heard it said that God's timing is perfect and He's never late, and that's true. But it's also true that He's usually not early, either! God often uses circumstances like these to stretch our faith, to encourage us to depend on Him for our needs, and to remind us of His faithfulness. I've learned from experience that when we make God our Source, He will move heaven and earth to provide what we need at just the right time. And why would we want to make anything or anyone else our source? Can our employers go ahead of us and supply our needs before they arise? Can our spouses, parents, or anyone else? The Bible says, "God will liberally supply (fill to the full) your every need according to His riches in glory in Christ Jesus" (Phil. 4:19 AMP). Only God can make

LIVE ON PURPOSE TODAY

To make sure you're a proper channel to receive *from* the Lord, means you must also make sure you're a proper channel to give *for* the Lord. Do you know someone who has a need today that God is asking you to meet? If not, ask Him where you can give today—knowing that, in turn, He will provide for you.

a promise like this, and He's not about to share His glory with anyone else. (Isa. 42:8.) If we're ever tempted to depend on our own wisdom or talents, or our money, the Lord has some stern warnings for us: "Your 'wisdom' and 'knowledge' have caused you to turn away from Me and claim, 'I am self-sufficient and not accountable to anyone!' So disaster will overtake you suddenly, and you won't be able to charm it away. Calamity will fall upon you and you won't be able to buy your way out. A catastrophe will arise so fast that you won't know what hit you" (Isa. 47:10,11 NLT). Just as the Lord went ahead of Abraham and provided the ram in the thicket to substitute for Isaac as a sacrifice, He will go ahead of us and provide exactly what we need at just the right time. I once heard a godly man say, "Don't stick the knife into Isaac until you look for the ram in the thicket." What that means to me is that if a need arises and we don't seek the Lord first for *His* wisdom and solution for it, we may make wrong decisions that can have devastating and far-reaching consequences. Experiences like this one that my family had reassure us that God truly is in control, and He is more than willing and able to fulfill our every need, if we'll let Him. Make Him your Source today, and give Him the chance to prove His faithfulness time and time again.

PRAYER

Lord, today I make You the Source of all my needs, committing them all to You. Help me to do my part by always seeking You and Your kingdom first. (Matt. 6:33.) When I'm tempted to trust in other people or things to supply my needs, remind me how that will only lead to disappointment and defeat. Thank You for proving Yourself faithful again and again!

Spirit-Led Prayer

> *The Spirit helps us in our weakness. We do not know what*
> *we ought to pray for, but the Spirit himself intercedes for us....*
> *The Spirit intercedes for the saints in accordance with God's will.*
>
> ROMANS 8:26,27

During the prayer request time at a meeting of his high
school Bible club, my son asked for prayer for his grandmother (my mother), who had just been diagnosed with
a suspicious growth in her body and was scheduled for a biopsy.
He was dismayed when the girl who was helping him lead the
club began by praying simply that any cancer found in my
mother's body would be treatable. Led by the Spirit of God, my
son followed with a prayer asking that absolutely no trace of
cancer would be found in his grandmother's body, and that she
would need no special treatment as a result of the biopsy findings.
We were all amazed when we heard a few days later that not only
was my mother cancer free, but the suspicious growth in her body
was a harmless mass of fatty tissue that required no further treatment. This experience taught us a valuable lesson about prayer. If
we let Him, the Holy Spirit will help us to pray God's will for ourselves and others, as the verses above promise. Best of all, our
Spirit-led prayers can invite God to do "exceedingly abundantly
above all we dare ask or imagine" in our lives and circumstances
(Eph. 3:20).

Recently, I read a testimony about a woman whose son was
in a serious car accident and was told by the doctors that he

would not survive. Overcome with grief, she prayed and asked God to spare her son's life, even if he was left severely crippled. Immediately, she was convicted by the Holy Spirit, who prompted her to pray for a complete recovery for her son. She obeyed, and as a result, her son was restored to wholeness in a way that even the doctors called "miraculous." I can't help but wonder how different things would have turned out for this woman and her family if she had not been sensitive to the Spirit of God's leading. She could have easily listened to and agreed with the negative reports that surrounded her, especially by the medical experts who had examined her son. She could have caved into her fears and feelings of desperation and despair. And she could have seen the visible damage done to her son's body and concluded—as most of us would have—that he was doomed. Instead, she boldly embraced God's invitation to lay hold of a miracle for her child. I believe that too often we let our minds, our circumstances, or other people tell us how to pray. As a result, we often settle for less than God's best. The Bible says, "The Lord is able to give you much more than this" (2 Chron. 25:9 NKJV). This is God's invitation to go from good to better, and from better to best in every area of our lives. Prayer is an essential part of the process, and that's why it's important for us to depend on God's Spirit to help us pray. Very often I'm prompted by the Holy Spirit to pray for the "impossible." Invariably, my own spirit cries out, "But

LIVE ON PURPOSE TODAY

Ask yourself where you have been making do with good instead of better and making do with better instead of best. Armed with those insights, begin a series of Spirit-led adjustments!

what if God doesn't answer my prayer?" The answer that always comes is, "What if He does?" I've decided that I'd rather ask and risk disappointment than to never know if the Lord would have used me to lay hold of a miracle for someone. What circumstances are you facing today that could use a touch of the miraculous? Today, ask the Lord to lead you in prayer, then get ready to reap an abundance of blessings!

PRAYER

Lord, teach me to ask for Your guidance when I pray for myself and others. Help me to become sensitive to Your Spirit's leading by seeking You daily in prayer, praise, and Bible study. Give me the faith and the grace I need to reach for Your highest and best in every situation. Thank You that my Spirit-led prayers will bless many and glorify You!

Keeping Our Dreams in Proper Perspective

Each one should use whatever gift he has received to serve others, faithfully administering God's grace in its various forms. If anyone serves, he should do it with the strength God provides, so that in all things God may be praised through Jesus Christ.

1 PETER 4:10,11

Several years ago I saw a famous Christian singer being interviewed on television. She was talking about how she had always wanted to reach millions for Christ with her musical talents and to glorify God with her popularity. Then she said something that really made an impression on me and that has stuck with me till this day. She said that she decided long ago that if the Lord didn't allow her dream to be fulfilled, she would just depend on Him to give her the grace to deal with it—and she would go on and enjoy her life just the same. What I admired most about this young woman was that she had the faith and the courage to put her dreams and desires "on the altar," and to leave them in God's hands. She admitted that she would have been sorely disappointed if her dreams didn't come to pass, but she refused to have a "do or die" attitude about her heartfelt desires, and she surrendered them to the Lord.

There's nothing wrong with having visions, dreams, and goals. God wants us to have these things. But He wants us to have goals that line up with His will for us. When we get into agreement with God's will and purposes for our lives, there's no devil in hell, no person on earth, that can stop them from coming to pass. In fact, the only one who can really stand between us and our God-given destiny is us. Satan can't. Our families can't. Our bosses can't. Even the government can't. No one can prevent us from becoming the man or woman of God that we were created to be. Except us. We can live our lives the way we want to, and we can turn our backs on God's perfect plans for us, if we so choose. And in the end, all we will have to show for it is regret. Or we can get in line with God's will for us, and we can watch Him unfold our lives like a beautiful flower, one petal at a time. We can do this by surrendering ourselves to the Lord—spirit, soul, and body—and by seeking Him and His will for us every day of our lives through prayer, devotion, and the study of His Word.

One thing I've learned from walking with the Lord these ten years is this: God will test our devotion to Him by letting us experience times of disappointment, especially where the fulfillment of our dreams is concerned. How we respond to these disappointments will help determine how much God can use us and bless us. If we respond with pouting, sulking, complaining, or threatening, God will have to treat us like the babies we're imitating, and He will not be able to trust us with the level of responsibility or blessing He longs to. But if we respond with an attitude that says—"God, I don't understand this, and it really hurts, but I

LIVE ON PURPOSE TODAY

Verbalize to yourself—or perhaps to a spouse or a best friend—new directions the Lord is speaking to your heart. Also share with this confidant how you will keep the Lord in first place as you pursue new direction.

believe that You are good, and You will work this out for my good"—the Lord will reward our faithfulness and spiritual maturity beyond our highest expectations. I recently heard a definition for *idol* that made me shudder. It said, "An idol is anything you feel you can't live without and be happy." It can be a dream, a desire, a thing, or even a person. The Bible says that our God is a jealous God, and He's not about to share us with anything or anyone else. (Ex. 20:5.) He expects our wholehearted devotion, and He deserves it, simply because He's God. If we ever find ourselves desiring something so much that we feel we can't live without it, God may close the door to it—either temporarily or permanently—depending on what He feels is best for our spiritual well-being. The Lord wants us to be able to say with all sincerity, "God, I can live without this dream—but I can't live without *You!*" With an attitude like this, we can walk in the awesome plans and purposes that God has mapped out for us, and we can have all the joy, peace, and fulfillment that are ours in Christ.

If God has closed a door on a heartfelt desire or dream of yours today, take comfort in the fact that He is saying to you one of two things. Either it's, "Wait. It's not the right time yet." Or, "I have something better for you." In either case, you can't lose, because you have put your trust in a God who loves you with a perfect love and who has your best interests at heart!

PRAYER

*Lord, show me Your will and purposes for my life, and help
me to make them my personal goals. Help me to always give
You first place in my life, so that everything else will fall into place.
When I experience disappointment and heartache, comfort me and
fill me with a fresh sense of hope. I can live without the things
of this world, Lord—but I can't live without You!*

Breaking Destructive Patterns

*People ruin their lives by their own foolishness
and then are angry at the Lord.*

PROVERBS 19:3 NLT

I recently heard from a woman who complained about all of the men she had been in relationship with who had lied, cheated, and mistreated her. She was completely disgusted, and she sounded bitter and resentful. She asked for prayer, that God would finally send her a decent man whom she could share her life with and who would be good to her. As I read her words, it didn't take long for me to figure out what this woman's real problem was. It wasn't men, in general. And it wasn't God. It was her. This woman was continually being hurt because she was continually out of God's will where her relationships were concerned. She was not being led by God's Spirit in choosing a partner, but she was being led by her own feelings and emotions. And as a result, her relationships with these men were doomed to fail.

Maybe you've known people like this woman. I certainly have. And maybe, like me, you've desperately tried to help them. Unfortunately, people like these who have displayed a pattern of failed relationships and destructive habits aren't likely to change just because we reach out to them. Scripture says, "A short-tempered man must bear his own penalty; you can't do much to help him. If you must try once, you must try a dozen times!" (Prov. 19:19 TLB). While this proverb refers to people who have a habit of losing their temper, the principle is the same for those who exhibit other destructive tendencies. Another proverb puts it like this: "As a dog returns to his vomit, so a fool repeats his folly" (Prov. 26:11 NLT). We can earnestly pray for these people, and we can give them sound advice when the Lord leads us to, but anything beyond that will most likely be a waste of time and energy on our part. What these people really need is a change of heart, and that's something that can only come from God. Sadly, God is often the last one that people like these will resort to.

What if you can identify with this woman yourself? I believe I have some godly advice for you today. First, focus on becoming the man or woman of God that you were created to be. The Lord is more likely to reward you with a loving and faithful mate if you are the kind of person who deserves such blessings from Him.

Proverbs says, "The man who finds a wife finds a good thing; she is a blessing to him from the Lord" (Prov. 18:22 TLB). God may have the perfect spouse all picked out for you, but He may first want to prepare you to receive this blessed relationship so that it has every chance of not only surviving, but thriving, when you finally come together. Use this period of waiting to nurture your relationship with God.

LIVE ON PURPOSE TODAY

The Lord will surely answer your request and reveal to you destructive patterns in your life and how to gain freedom. As He does, search God's Word for Scriptures that promise freedom from your destructive ways and meditate wholly upon them. They will bring you the strength to forge a new path.

Jesus said, "Seek first His kingdom and His righteousness, and all these things will be given to you as well" (Matt. 6:33). Putting God first in our lives can have a positive impact on every area of our lives, even where our relationships are concerned. Secondly, trust God to bring the right mate for you at just the right time. Most people don't realize how critical this is, and because of that, they get involved with relationships that God never meant for them to. Realize that by involving yourself in the wrong relationships, you could be delaying or forfeiting the ideal one that God has destined for you.

Benjamin Franklin said, "The definition of insanity is doing the same thing over and over and expecting different results." When we've established a pattern that isn't working, we can call on the Lord to help us break that destructive pattern once and for all. When we do, we can rest assured that all the help of heaven will be on our side!

PRAYER

Lord, do a new work in my heart and life now so that I will begin to focus on becoming all You created me to be. Help me to wholeheartedly trust You to bring the right relationships into my life at just the right time. Please reveal to me any destructive patterns that I might have in my life today, and show me how to gain the freedom that is mine in Christ. Thank You, Lord, that no matter how badly I've failed in the past, I can begin to walk in victory as I give You first place in my life!

When Words Are Many

When words are many, sin is not absent,
but he who holds his tongue is wise.

PROVERBS 10:19

When I began seriously studying the Bible some years
ago, I was amazed at how many verses warned
against talking too much. It never occurred to me that
being too talkative could lead us into sin. But the above verse
makes it clear that it can. Proverbs 10:14 TLB says, "A wise man
holds his tongue. Only a fool blurts out everything he knows;
that only leads to sorrow and trouble." The fact is, the more we
talk, the more likely we are to say something that we will be
sorry for later. And just like we can't "un-ring a bell," we can't
ever take back the words we've spoken. We can apologize for
them or try to correct them, but once they are out of our mouths,
we must live with the consequences of them. Proverbs 17:28 NLT
says, "Even fools are thought to be wise when they keep silent;
when they keep their mouths shut, they seem intelligent." It's
tempting sometimes to attempt to display our knowledge about
something, especially if we want to impress someone, but the
truth is that often we'll seem more wise and make a better
impression if we talk less. We ourselves determine whether our
lips will be a blessing to us or a curse. Proverbs 18:7 NLT says,
"The mouths of fools are their ruin; their lips get them into
trouble." Notice it doesn't say "their ears get them into trouble."
We'd get into a lot less trouble if we did more listening and less
talking. If we're ever tempted to believe that what comes out of

our mouths isn't important, we need only to remember Proverbs 13:3: "He who guards his lips guards his life."

God gives us a command in James 1:19 that can change our lives for the better, if we choose to live by it: "Everyone should be quick to listen, slow to speak, and slow to become angry." It's important to the Lord that we listen to others. It's one of the best ways to show someone that we love and respect them. We are being selfish and arrogant when we monopolize a conversation and do most of the talking, giving others the impression that what they might have to say is of little importance to us. Besides that, we lose many opportunities for gaining wisdom and getting to know others better when we're talking instead of listening to what they have to contribute to the conversation. It takes a lot of humility to be a good listener, but it's a goal worth striving for because it pleases God, blesses others, and rewards us in the long run. Sometimes when we've dominated the conversation and others present have even encouraged us to do so, we can get the impression that we did the right thing. But chances are that afterwards our captive audience will criticize us behind our backs and actually dread a similar experience with us in the future. I have seen the consequences of excessive talking, and they can be devastating. That shouldn't really surprise us, though, because if it's displeasing to God, it cannot bear good fruit, only bad. Yes,

LIVE ON PURPOSE TODAY

Make it your goal to listen well and talk less. Since the Bible says a truly wise man or woman uses few words, use as few as you can today. And you'll be the wiser for it!

there are times we need to do the speaking. Ecclesiastes 3:7 says there is "a time to be silent and a time to speak." We need to offer our lips to the Lord each day and ask Him to make us sensitive to the leading of His Spirit in this area. I often like to pray as David did in Psalm 141:3, "Set a guard over my mouth, O Lord; keep watch over the door of my lips" (Ps. 141:3). Today, may the Lord deeply plant in our hearts the truth that, "A truly wise person uses few words" (Prov. 17:27 NLT).

PRAYER

Lord, teach me to be a good listener. Help me to be more giving and generous when I'm conversing with others. When I'm tempted to talk too much, convict me by Your Spirit; remind me that I'm displeasing You, and no good can come from it. Thank You that as a result, I'll enjoy richer relationships with You and others!

Good Reason To Hope

We have this hope as an anchor for the soul, firm and secure.

HEBREWS 6:19

The last time I went through a dark and difficult period in my life, the Lord showed me this verse and gave me new and valuable insight through it. He showed me how I could remain more stable during trials and tribulations if I would purposefully place my hope in Him and His Word, allowing that hope to act as an anchor for my soul. As He reminded me that our soul is made up of our mind, will, and emotions, I began to understand how learning the principles in this verse could make me more stable and help me avoid being tossed to and fro by the people and circumstances surrounding me.

We could all benefit from using some positive self-talk the way the psalmist often did. Psalm 43:5 says, "Why are you downcast, O my soul? Why so disturbed within me? Put your hope in God, for I will yet praise him, my Savior and my God." The author is talking to the soulish part of himself here, saying that by placing his hope firmly in God, he will find relief from discouragement and despair. In Psalm 27:13 NASB, David writes, "I would have despaired unless I had believed that I would see the goodness of the Lord in the land of the living." Notice that David didn't have to actually see God's goodness before he found relief from despair; he only had to *believe* he would see it, and that was enough. Perhaps when you're going through difficult times, you find it hard to believe. I can relate to that. But recently, God led me to some wonderful insights from a godly man who said that if we think of faith as a *choice* rather than an *ability,* we will understand that faith is actually simpler than it seems. And we can ask the Lord to help us to make that choice. Psalm 31:24 NKJV says, "Be of good courage, and He shall strengthen your heart, all you who hope in the Lord." As we do our part by making the decision to take our stand in faith and to place our hope in God, He has promised to do His part by strengthening us and helping us stand firm till the victory comes.

Look at the role that hope plays in the psalmist's prayer in Psalm 33:22, "May Your unfailing love rest upon us, O Lord, even as we put our hope in You." The author is saying here, "Bless us to the same degree that we put our hope in You, Lord." The Amplified translation says it best: "Let Your mercy and loving-kindness, O Lord, be upon us in proportion to our waiting and hoping for You." The Bible makes it clear that God is pleased when we place our hope in Him and His goodness, and He is eager to reward us when we do. Psalm 33:18-19 says, "The eyes of the Lord are on those who fear Him, on those whose hope is in

LIVE ON PURPOSE TODAY

If you are facing difficult times, search the Bible today for Scriptures that promise your deliverance. Commit them to memory and cling to them—for securing hope in God's Word is to secure hope in God!

His unfailing love, to deliver them from death and keep them alive in famine." This is God's promise of protection and provision to those who choose to put their trust in Him in times of adversity. As long as I can remember, I have always believed in God. But it wasn't until I began devoting myself to His Word that I had something tangible that I could hang on to when times got rough. I can easily relate to the psalmist's sentiment when he says, "Your Word is my only source of hope" (Ps. 119:114 NLT). There have been many times when my faith was stretched to the limit, and all I could do was cling to God's promise in Isaiah 49:23: "Those who hope in Me will not be disappointed." I can't promise that every time you place your hope in God, things will turn out exactly the way you want them to. But I can promise you that every time you choose to hope instead of doubt, the Lord will honor your faith somehow. And that is why I urge you today—"Wait for God. Wait with hope. Hope now; hope always!" (Ps. 131:3 MESSAGE).

PRAYER

Lord, teach me how to be more stable in difficult times. Reveal to me how putting my hope in You, Your Word, and Your goodness will open the door for me to receive all the blessings You have in store for me. Remind me how maintaining a hopeful attitude can be the best antidote for discouragement and despair. Thank You that as I do my part in gaining the victory, You will do Yours!

The Lord Can Give You Much More

{ *The Lord can give you much more than that.* }

2 CHRONICLES 25:9

When my sons were teenagers, we went to our local Christian bookstore one evening because they were having a contest and giving away numerous prizes. The grand prize was a huge Christian music collection. My boys entered their names and prayed that they would win. As it turned out, they didn't win. But later that night, the store owner shared a remarkable story with us about the winner that inspired my sons and gave them consolation. The young man who won the contest was a new believer in Christ, and just a few nights before, he had thrown out his entire collection of secular music, vowing to listen only to music that glorified His Savior. The Lord used this contest to reward him with an entire new collection of music that he could enjoy with God's blessing.

This experience reminded me of the biblical account of King Amaziah of Judah. When the king was organizing his army, he paid $200,000 to hire 100,000 experienced mercenaries to fight alongside his own troops in battle. Then a prophet of God told Amaziah that no matter how well his army fought, the Lord would not grant Him victory as long as he was making unrighteous alliances. The king's response to this news was—"But the money! What shall I do about that?" The prophet replied, "The Lord is able to give you much more than this!" (2 Chron. 2:9

TLB). Amaziah wisely chose to obey God in the matter, and he dismissed the mercenaries, sending them home with their pay. And the Lord rewarded the king's obedience with a great victory in battle. (2 Chron. 25:11,12.)

Both Amaziah and the young man who won the Christian music contest were faced with difficult choices. Both of them stood to lose a lot if they chose to obey God. Neither of them had any tangible proof ahead of time that they would be rewarded for their obedience. But their decisions proved that they truly believed that if God asked them to give something up, He had something even better for them in mind.

The truth is that whenever we choose to do God's will, we can't lose—we can only gain. Jesus made this clear when He said, "I tell you the truth, no one who has left home or brothers or sisters or mother or father or children or fields for Me and the Gospel will fail to receive a hundred times as much in this present age...and in the age to come, eternal life" (Mark 10:29,30). Whenever we sacrifice relationships, material things, or anything else in order to please God, He will always make sure that we come out ahead in the end. God is not a taker; He's a giver. Once we get a revelation of this fact, we will be quick to make the sacrifices the Lord asks us to, knowing that it will be best for us in

LIVE ON PURPOSE TODAY

You've just prayed and asked the Lord to reveal anything hindering your relationship with Him. So, He's talking even now. Listen carefully, and then see how quickly you can act on what He says!

the end. But being blessed shouldn't be our main motivation for obeying God in situations like these. We should want to please God simply because we love Him, and because we want to show our gratitude for all He is and all He does. The apostle Paul had the right idea when he penned these words in the Book of Philippians: "But all these things that I once thought very worthwhile—now I've thrown them all away so that I can put my trust and hope in Christ alone. Yes, everything else is worthless when compared with the priceless gain of knowing Christ Jesus my Lord. I have put aside all else, counting it worth less than nothing, in order that I can have Christ, and become one with Him..." (Phil. 3:7-9 TLB). Paul didn't want anything to come between Him and God, and we should have the same attitude. What is it that's standing between you and a deeper, more intimate relationship with the Lord? Talk to Him about it today. And believe that no matter what your obedience may cost you, the Lord has something better waiting for you up ahead!

PRAYER

Lord, I ask that You reveal to me today anything that is hindering me from having a more vibrant relationship with You. Help me to make the sacrifices I need to make so that I can become all You want me to be and receive all You want me to have. Thank You for transforming all of my "losses" into gains!

The Power of Joy

{ *Don't be dejected and sad, for the joy
of the Lord is your strength!*

NEHEMIAH 8:10 NLT }

When I was going through a very difficult time recently and praying for strength, the Lord showed me the above verse. I had read it countless times before, but this time it shed new light on a simple truth for me. In order for us to be truly strong in spirit, the way God wants us to be, we must be filled with His joy. If you don't believe this is true, the next time you begin to feel weak or weary, check your joy level. Chances are that it will be way down. The kind of joy I'm speaking about is not the worldly "feel good" kind, but it's a deep, abiding joy born of the Holy Spirit. The Bible says that joy is a fruit of the Spirit. (Gal. 5:22.) All believers have the "seed" of joy planted in our spirits, and it's up to us to cooperate with God to develop it and help it grow. One way we can do that is by praying for joy. Once I began reading the Scriptures and discovering that I had a God-given right to be filled with His joy, I began praying for it confidently, based on 1 John 5:14-15, which says that when we pray according to the will of God, we will receive what we ask for. David confirms that praying for joy is scriptural when he writes, "Bring joy to Your servant, for to You, O Lord, I lift up my soul" (Ps. 86:4).

Jesus said that answered prayer can be a source of joy. He tells us, "Ask, using My name, and you will receive, and your cup of joy will overflow" (John 16:24). I have found that the more I pray, the more blessings I receive, and the more my joy abounds. Another way to cultivate the seed of joy in us is to encourage ourselves with God's truth and promises. Psalm 119:162 says, "I rejoice in Your promise like one who finds great spoil." Some translations say "great treasure." If you've ever gone through a trial and had nothing to hang on to but a promise from God, like I have, you know how precious His Word can be, and how much joy it can bring to a troubled heart. Spending time in God's presence is another way of increasing our joy. David wrote, "You will fill me with joy in Your presence" (Ps. 16:11). There's simply no substitute for spending time with God in prayer, praise, and Bible reading. That's when He imparts to us His wisdom, peace, joy, and strength. When we neglect to spend quality time with God, our burdens become unbearable and our joy diminishes.

Jesus made it clear that joy was God's will for us. He said that He wanted the "full measure" of His joy to be in us (John 17:13). And He said that He desired that our joy would be "complete" (John 15:11). The Savior wasn't talking about a fleeting sense of happiness here, but one that

LIVE ON PURPOSE TODAY

Encourage yourself with God's truth and promises today. In fact, double up on your time in the Bible—it's guaranteed to stir up your joy and put a smile on your face!

would endure in the face of adversity. That's why He told us, "Here on earth you will have many trials and sorrows; but cheer up, for I have overcome the world" (John 16:33 TLB). The Amplified Bible goes on to say, "I have deprived it of power to harm you and have conquered it for you." He also said, "No one will take away your joy" (John 16:22). Jesus has made a way for us to have the joy of the Lord in a trouble-filled world. But it's up to us to do our part by nurturing our joy, and by refusing to surrender it to the enemy. Satan works overtime trying to steal our joy because he knows that it makes us strong and difficult to defeat. He also knows that he can seriously damage our witness and our effectiveness as believers if he can keep us sad, sour, and sullen.

Maybe you've heard the old saying, "Laughter is the best medicine." There's actually a scriptural basis for this truth. Proverbs 17:22 NASB says, "A joyful heart is good medicine." Even much of today's scientific and medical community will acknowledge that there is a direct connection between our joy level and our health and well-being. The Bible says that we should be "filled with an inexpressible and glorious joy" as the result of our faith in Jesus and our love for Him (1 Peter 1:8). God deserves cheerful servants, and it should be our goal to worship and serve Him with joy. (Ps. 100:2.) Finally, nothing brings more joy to our hearts than placing our wholehearted trust in God, especially in times of trouble. (Rom. 15:13.) If you are facing challenging circumstances today and have lost your joy in the Lord, you may be handing your blessings and your well-being over to the enemy on a silver platter. Don't do it. Hang on to your joy till the victory comes, trusting that the Lord's strength will be there for you every step of the way!

PRAYER

Lord, fill me with Your joy to give me strength. Show me how to have the kind of joy that draws others to You. When the enemy comes against me and I'm tempted to lose my joy, remind me of what it can cost me. Thank You that Your joy shall remain in me and overflow!

Hearing the Good Shepherd's Voice

{ *My sheep hear My voice and I know them, and they follow Me.* }

JOHN 10:27 NKJV

One night a few years ago, my son John began experiencing such severe abdominal pain that my husband and I had to take him to the hospital. Almost as soon as we arrived at the emergency room, things began happening much too fast. A parade of doctors and nurses examined John, and before we knew it a surgeon was being called in. It was recommended that my son not be allowed to go home that night, but that he be admitted to the hospital for further treatment. In the middle of all the activity and noise, I got quiet in my spirit and pleaded with the Lord to show me what to do. I literally tuned out all the voices around me and focused my mind and heart on hearing God's "still, small voice." After making a decision, I approached my husband and convinced him to help me get our son out of there as quickly as possible. The doctors and nurses shook their heads and gave us stern warnings. Even so, we signed the necessary papers to get John released and to give up our rights to hold the hospital responsible if he was harmed as a result. And we took our son home.

After praying and seeking God, I began to believe that John was experiencing a drug reaction from the medicine our doctor had given him days before for an infection. The day after the hospital incident I called our family doctor (who was not available the night before), and I told him what had transpired. He confirmed that I handled the situation perfectly, and that it was likely that John's medicine was in fact the problem. When word got around to our family and friends about the incident, some of them chastised me for taking John out of the hospital against the staff's advice and for taking risks with my son's welfare. After doing some soul-searching, I decided to trust that I had heard from God when I initially sought His guidance in the matter. Once John was off the offending drug, his health began to improve dramatically, and we praised and thanked God for His faithfulness.

The longer I walk with the Lord, the more I realize how much He wants us to be able to hear and heed His voice. Jesus said, "My sheep hear My voice and I know them, and they follow Me" (John 10:27 NKJV). But I've also noticed that sometimes my circumstances, past experiences, or other people can speak louder to me than God does. That's why it's so important for us to make an effort to avoid the things that can hinder our hearing from the Lord. And that's why it's essential for us to have a "right heart" before God at all times. Bitterness, anger, and resentment will make it difficult for us to tune in to God's voice. So will

LIVE ON PURPOSE TODAY

Nurture a more intimate relationship with the Father by setting time aside today to spend with Him. Enter into His gates with thanksgiving, into His courts with praise—and then remain in the throne room to commune with Him.

unconfessed sin. One thing that helps me to stay right with God is the fear that I won't be able to receive His perfect wisdom and guidance when my loved ones and I are in a crisis situation. It's just not worth it for me to harbor ill-feelings toward anyone, or to stubbornly remain unrepentant when I sin. Another way we can hinder our communication with God is to live a constantly busy and hurried lifestyle. It's true that we don't always have to get alone and quiet before God in order to hear from Him. But it's also true that there are some distinct advantages to doing that, because when we're communing with the Lord "on the run," we will do most of the talking. Because God usually speaks to us in a "gentle whisper" (1 Kings 19:12), it's important for us to continually sharpen our listening skills in a spiritual sense. We can do that by seeking the Lord daily in prayer and Bible reading. Renewing our minds with the truth of God's Word will make us more sensitive to His voice and more resistant to Satan's deceptions. Also, we must expect God to speak to us and *believe* that we can hear from Him, thereby exercising our faith to be led by His Spirit. Every day I declare, "I hear the voice of the Good Shepherd and I do follow Him." As I stand on this promise and seek Him daily, I gain the confidence I need to receive His guidance by faith. Hearing from God is not mysterious or spooky—it's scriptural. And it's necessary if we're going to fulfill our God-given purpose in this life. Today, trust that the Lord wants to speak to your heart, and say to Him—as Samuel did—"Speak, Lord, Your servant is listening!" (1 Sam. 3:9).

PRAYER

Lord, teach me how to tune in to Your voice and to tune out the voices that are not of You. Show me how to maintain a right heart before You always. Help me to do my part in nurturing a more intimate relationship with You so that I can become more sensitive to Your voice. Thank You for giving me the confidence I need to hear and follow You!

Cast Those Cares

Cast your cares on the Lord and he will sustain you;
he will never let the righteous fall.

PSALM 55:22

"Sustain" is a great word. If you look it up in the dictionary, the definition says: "To provide for the support of; specifically to provide sustenance or nourishment for; carry the weight or burden of."[2] God is promising us in the verse above that if we will do our part by casting our cares upon Him, He will do His part by sustaining us. I think that's a pretty good deal, don't you? But let's be honest here. Casting our cares on the Lord isn't always as easy as it sounds. Even when we sincerely want to hand our burdens over to God, we often can't. Many times we're left struggling with burdens God never meant for us to handle. The results are often anxiety, depression, despair, and even sickness and infirmity. But maybe I can help convince you that God really does want to carry your burdens and that it's worth the effort to surrender them to Him. In 1 Peter 5:7 NLT, the apostle Peter restates the verse above: "Give all your worries and cares to God, for he cares about what happens to you." It's because God cares—and because He never created you to shoulder your burdens alone—that He wants you to give Him all your worries. Only God's shoulders are big enough to carry our daily concerns. Ours aren't. Look at this promise in Psalm 68:19: "Praise be to the Lord, to God our Savior, who daily bears our burdens." All these verses make it clear that God wants to bear *all* our cares *all* the time.

In Luke 21:34-35 TLB, Jesus gives us this stern warning: "Watch out! Don't let my sudden coming catch you unaware; don't let me find you...occupied with the problems of this life, like all the rest of the world." And in Mark 4:19, Jesus says that "the worries of this life" can actually "choke the word [of God], making it unfruitful" in our lives. Instead, the Savior tells us, "Come to me, all of you who are weary and carry heavy burdens, and I will give you rest. Take my yoke upon you. Let me teach you, because I am humble and gentle, and you will find rest for your souls. For my yoke fits perfectly, and the burden I give you is light" (Matt. 11:28-30 NLT). If we let the Savior teach us His way of handling the affairs of this life, we will find the rest and relief He so graciously offers. It's the Lord's sincere desire that we give all our cares to Him, but He won't wrestle them away from us. We must surrender them to Him, trusting that He has our best interests at heart. When we do, we open the door for God to work wonders in our circumstances and lives. Each day, tell the Lord, "I give You all my cares and burdens, Lord. Thank You for sustaining me, according to Your promise." You can be specific, naming your cares if you want to. Then when worry or doubt come against you, say, "Lord, I thank You that You're taking care of that for me!" And let the peace of God quiet your heart and mind. May this precious promise from God encourage you today: "I

LIVE ON PURPOSE TODAY

Cast your cares on the Lord today in a way you won't soon forget. Stretch one hand out in front of you. With the other hand, imagine that you pick up your care and deposit it in the outstretched hand. Now hand it up to the Lord—and be done with it once and for all!

will be your God through all your lifetime, yes, even when your hair is white with age. I made you and I will care for you. I will carry you along and be your Savior"! (Isa. 46:4 TLB).

PRAYER

Lord, today I cast all my cares upon You. When I'm tempted to carry my own burdens, remind me that Your will is for me to surrender them to You. Give me a new awareness of Your ability and willingness to solve my problems and handle my affairs. Thank You for rewarding me with rest and relief!

Faith Is Spelled "R-I-S-K"

{ *These were all commended for their faith, yet none of them received what had been promised.* }

HEBREWS 11:39

It always amazes me how many believers are hesitant to claim God's promises because they're afraid they'll be disappointed. Perhaps they feel that if they don't expect too much from God, they can avoid the pain of being let down. I've heard it said that real faith is spelled "R-I-S-K." I think there's a lot of truth to that. It takes a lot of courage to trust God to come through for us when our senses aren't giving us any support. But that's exactly what the Lord expects from us. If you look at the eleventh chapter of Hebrews, you see that God approves of those who put their faith in His promises, whether or not they come to pass. The verse above confirms this. And so does Hebrews 11:13: "All these people were still living by faith when they died. They did not receive the things promised; they only saw them and welcomed them from a distance." The Scriptures reveal that God holds in high esteem those who live by faith and continue to hold on to God's promises, even through long periods of waiting. The fact is, if we really want to please God and reap the rewards He has in store for us, we're going to have to risk putting our faith and trust in Him, even when it looks like the odds are against us. Hebrews 11:6 tells us that, "Without faith it is impossible to please God, because anyone who comes to Him must believe that He exists, and that He rewards those who earnestly seek Him."

The first verse of Hebrews gives us a biblical definition of faith: "Now faith is being sure of what we hope for and certain of what we do not see." And the next verse reveals that it's this kind of faith that God esteems: "This is what the ancients were commended for" (Heb. 11:1,2). The words "sure" and "certain" make it clear that faith is a confidence in God and His Word, even when we don't see any tangible evidence to justify that faith. And the verse that follows reveals why our believing in what we don't see isn't just "pie in the sky": "By faith we understand that the universe was formed at God's command, so that what is seen was not made out of what was visible" (Heb. 11:3). The Creator of the universe isn't the least bit hindered when our circumstances look "impossible." Making something out of nothing is what our God does best. Now you need to ask yourself how serious you are about pleasing God. If you're really serious, you aren't going to be able to avoid taking risks with your faith. Yes, you're going to experience some disappointments you might have escaped. But I guarantee you this—you're going to witness some miracles in your life that you would have otherwise missed. Hebrews 11:33 tells us that "through faith" some of God's people "gained what was promised." The bottom line is this—whether or not we receive all the promises we

LIVE ON PURPOSE TODAY

Apply your faith to any need you face today. Find a Scripture that promises your answer, take hold of it by faith, and then thank God for His gracious supply. Give God the opportunity to do what He does best— and make something out of nothing for you!

believe God for isn't the issue; the issue is whether or not we are living by faith, trusting God with all our hearts in every circumstance every day of our lives. When we do, along with God's hearty approval, we'll have a peace and joy in our hearts that will enable us to live the abundant life that Jesus came to give us. Today, my heartfelt prayer for you is that you'll *dare to believe!*

PRAYER

Lord, forgive me for the times I've missed Your perfect will because I was fearful or timid. Give me a holy boldness that will dare to believe in Your promises and risk disappointment. Help me to keep my eyes on You and Your Word, instead of on my circumstances. Thank You that as I live by faith each day, I'll impact the lives of others with my peace and joy!

By the Obedience of One

For as by one man's disobedience many were made sinners,
so by the obedience of one shall many be made righteous.

ROMANS 5:15 KJV

This verse, written by the apostle Paul, has special meaning for me. I can still remember the day the Lord showed it to me in a fresh new way. I was feeling very discouraged over the lack of faith of several of my loved ones, and I was pouring my heart out to the Lord, lamenting over my powerlessness to make a difference. He led me to this Scripture, and it fairly leapt off the page into my heart. It became God's special promise to me that if I would just concentrate on devoting myself to Him and focusing on my own behavior, He would honor and reward my obedience by using me to impact my loved ones and draw them to Him.

Proverbs 10:17 says, "He who heeds discipline shows the way to life, but whoever ignores correction leads others astray." The devil will try to convince us that it doesn't matter how we live, but the Bible says otherwise. Each day, by our actions we choose to influence others in a positive or negative way. The Amplified Bible puts it this way: "He who heeds instruction and correction is [not only himself] in the way of life [but also] is a way of life for others. And he who neglects or refuses reproof [not only himself] goes astray [but also] causes to err and is a path toward ruin for others" (Prov. 10:17 AMP). Just as we can do others a lot of good by living disciplined lives wholly devoted to the Lord, we can also do them a lot of harm by living "sloppy" lives. When you say that to some Christians, they bristle, because they simply don't want to be held accountable to that extent. But whether they like it or not, God sees them as role models, and they will answer to Him for their selfishness and lack of concern for their fellow man. Instead of seeing this responsibility as a burden, believers should rejoice that they have God-given power to make a real difference in this world for His glory. Job 22:30 says, "He will deliver even one who is not innocent, who will be delivered through the cleanness of your hands." We don't have to be perfect to have the "clean hands" that Scripture refers to here. We just need to have a heart that is bent toward God's will—a heart that wants above all else to please Him. Then the Lord will save even those who are "not innocent," simply because of our devotion to Him.

James 5:16 NLT says, "The earnest prayer of a righteous person has great power and wonderful results." It's easy for us to doubt the truth of this verse when we have prayed and stood in faith for someone's salvation and deliverance, and have seen little to encourage us. But God doesn't want us to depend on what we

LIVE ON PURPOSE TODAY

If you've laid aside prayers for friends and family members out of discouragement, purpose today to pick them back up. Your prayers can make a difference!

discern through our five senses. He wants us to go deeper than that, and to firmly believe and hope in His Word. If you have trusted Christ as your Lord and Savior, your prayers have immeasurable power. Satan wants you to doubt that, though, because if you don't, you will persevere in prayer and eventually see the evidence of your prayer power. One of the main reasons why we don't see a greater move of the Spirit of God in the lives of others is because most Christians lose heart and give up before they see the answers to their prayers and the fulfillment of God's promises. I have a relative whom I have prayed for and ministered to for years, and who has persisted in unbelief and bitterness toward God and others. Recently, I got so disgusted that I decided I would continue to pray for her, but to do no more than that. I was astonished when shortly afterwards she began telling me about all the wonderful biblical teaching she was listening to and being blessed by. These radical changes in my loved one seemed to come "out of the blue." But the truth is that they were a direct result of the multitude of prayers I said for her and my determination to set a Christlike example for her.

If there are some loved ones in your life whom you long to see saved and delivered, please know that "by the obedience of one," many can be "made righteous." You can make a difference in your family, your school, and your workplace. If you will just concentrate on serving the Lord with all your heart, and glorifying Him with your daily life, He will honor your obedience by using you in mighty ways to lead multitudes to Him!

PRAYER

Lord, I thank You for giving me the privilege and the power to touch and change lives for Your glory. Today, I renew my commitment to love and serve You with all my heart, soul, mind, and strength. Thank You for using me in new and exciting ways for Your glory as I walk in obedience to You!

Who Needs Signs?

While the harpist was playing, the hand of the Lord came upon
Elisha and he said, "This is what the Lord says: Make this
valley full of ditches. For this is what the Lord says: You will
see neither wind nor rain, yet this valley will be filled with
water, and you, your cattle and your other animals will
drink. This is an easy thing in the eyes of the Lord...."

2 KINGS 3:16-18

The kings of Israel, Judah, and Edom had united to attack
Moab. After a seven-day march, the army had no water left
for themselves or their animals. Their situation looked
hopeless, and they were prepared to die. Then good King
Jehoshaphat summoned Elisha, the prophet of God, who revealed
the Lord's plan to perform a miracle on their behalf. To me, the
most amazing part of this prophecy is the Lord saying, "You will
see neither wind nor rain...." God is saying here, "You're not
going to see any signs that a miracle is coming, but it's coming
just the same." And not only was God going to do something that
was virtually impossible, but He said, "This is an *easy* thing in the
eyes of the Lord"!

I can think of so many times that I encountered challenges in
my life—and though a part of me hoped God would intervene on
my behalf—my faith faltered because I thought, *I don't see any signs*
that He's doing anything! Are you waiting to see some evidence that
God is working on your behalf in a situation? Are you waiting for
the right phone call, letter in the mail, or other tangible evidence?

LIVE ON PURPOSE TODAY

Believing that your deliverance is on the way with or without signs, lift your hands toward heaven and thank God for His goodness, for His mercy that endures forever, and for His mighty power at work in your behalf!

Rest assured that it is an easy thing for God to come to your aid, even when signs that He will do so are virtually nonexistent!

PRAYER

Lord, forgive me when I've doubted You because I couldn't see any signs that You had plans to help me. Remind me that Your power and wisdom transcend my comprehension, and that Your love for me knows no bounds. Thank You that my deliverance is on its way—with or without signs!

A Message of Restoration

*I will repay you for the years the locusts have eaten...
and you will praise the name of the Lord
your God who has worked wonders for you.*

JOEL 2:25,26

These verses in the Bible have special meaning for me because I didn't become serious about my relationship with God until I was almost 40 years old. There have been many times when I've lamented over the fact that my children weren't raised in a true Christian home from the time they were born. And I've often regretted that my relationship with my husband and our marriage didn't get off on the right foot because of our lack of devotion to the Lord from the very beginning. If I allowed myself to dwell on things like these, I could come up with a multitude of regrets. Thankfully, God gave me these verses as a personal promise that He would work wonders for me by restoring the blessings I forfeited during all those years I was living for myself instead of Him. And He's been true to His Word. As I live this new life in Christ daily, I am continually amazed by the marvelous works of restoration that the Lord performs for me and my loved ones on a regular basis.

If you'll ask the Lord to reveal Himself to you as the God of restoration, He will restore things in your life that you thought were lost forever. I've seen Him restore broken families and relationships. I've also seen Him breathe new life into lost dreams and visions. And I've witnessed His miraculous power working in

LIVE ON PURPOSE TODAY

As God begins the work of restoration in your life, begin to pick up things you thought were lost forever—goals, dreams, talents, even friendships and relationships. As the Holy Spirit guides you, demonstrate fervor as if not even one day had slipped by.

people's lives to restore their health and finances. But I think the things He restores that mean the most to me are our faith, joy, peace, and hope. The Bible makes it abundantly clear—our God is in the restoration business. And my life and the lives of many others are living proof. If you're a child of the King, you don't have to assume that all the losses that come your way are set in stone. If you'll give the Lord a chance to have the final word, you'll be amazed at what He can do to make your whole life shiny and new!

PRAYER

Lord, today I believe and receive Your precious promises of restoration. I ask that You work wonders in my life by transforming my losses into blessings. Help me to do my part by seeking You daily and putting my trust in You. Thank You for making my whole life bright and beautiful for Your glory!

Rejoicing in Our Labor

To enjoy your work and accept your lot in life—
that is indeed a gift from God.

ECCLESIASTES 5:19 NLT

O ver the years I had read this verse many times, but about a month ago the Lord began shedding some new light on it for me. For as long as I can remember, I had this notion that I shouldn't expect to enjoy my work, and that I should approach much of my labor with a "grin and bear it" kind of attitude. And what was to convince me otherwise? It seemed that I was always surrounded by people who shared and demonstrated that exact mindset. But recently, the Lord began showing me the above verse and others like them, and dealing with me about my wrong thinking in this area. He led me to begin praying and standing on these truths for myself and my loved ones, and He has already begun to reward my faith with exciting new work-related blessings for all of us.

The Bible makes it abundantly clear that God wants us to enjoy our work. Solomon puts it plainly when he says, "To enjoy your work...that is indeed a gift from God" (Eccl. 5:19 NLT). This is a common theme throughout the Book of Ecclesiastes. Solomon also writes, "That everyone may eat and drink, and find satisfaction in all his toil—this is the gift of God" (Eccl. 3:13). So now that we know that God wants us to find joy and satisfaction in our work—and that these are gifts from Him—what can we do? We can ask Him for them, trusting that He is true to His Word when

He says that whenever we pray in line with His will, He will answer us. (1 John 5:14,15.) Jesus said, "If you, then, though you are evil, know how to give good gifts to your children, how much more will your Father in heaven give good gifts to those who ask him!" (Matt. 7:11). And James wrote, "You do not have, because you do not ask God" (James 4:2). The key word in these verses is *ask*. Don't assume that you have to settle for doing distasteful and unfulfilling work all your life. Yes, there may be times when we might have to endure some periods of doing work we dislike, but our prayer and our goal should be to spend most of our lives doing the kind of work that gives us joy. One of my regular prayers for myself and my family is, "Lord, please enable us to earn a good living doing what we love to do most." I also pray that God will help us to do our part in the fulfillment of this prayer. One way we can cooperate with the Lord to this end is to seek His guidance daily, depending on Him to keep us in His perfect will. When we're doing what God has called us to do, we will experience a peace, joy, and satisfaction that will be missing when we're out of His will.

LIVE ON PURPOSE TODAY

Enjoying your work is, indeed, a gift from God. So, graciously accept the Lord's gift and begin thanking Him for the reality of it to come to pass in your life!

I encourage you to begin asking God to make a way for you to enjoy your work. If you're in a position where you really dislike your job or the work you're doing, the Lord can open up a new door of opportunity for you as a result of your prayers. If it's not His will and timing for you to make a move right now, He can make your present job more pleasant and fulfilling somehow. He may do that by causing you to find favor or recognition in the sight of your employer or coworkers. Or He may improve your working conditions in various little ways until He can move you into a more desirable position. But rest assured that as you pray in faith, God will do *something* to enable you to enjoy your labor more. If you're a child of God, you don't have to resign yourself to a "grin and bear it" attitude toward your work. God has made a way for you to find joy and satisfaction in your toil. May you begin today to press on toward the goal of "rejoicing in your labor"! (Eccl. 5:19 NKJV).

PRAYER

Lord, I believe that it's Your will for me to enjoy my work.
Please teach me how to do that. Keep me in Your perfect
will so that I'll always be in the right place at the right time,
even where my work is concerned. Thank You for enabling
me to earn a good living doing what I love to do!

Equipped for Service

Each one should use whatever gift he has received to serve others,
faithfully administering God's grace in its various forms. If
anyone serves, he should do it with the strength God provides,
so that in all things God may be praised through Jesus Christ.

1 PETER 4:10,11

When my son started a Bible club at his high school, I offered to help out by driving home every student who needed a ride after the weekly meetings. I didn't want a single student to miss out on attending simply because they lacked transportation. Because I was a stay-at-home mom and my son was leading the club, I felt it was my duty to lend my assistance somehow. Every week I made several trips between the school and the students' homes, filling up my car each time. Often I was on the road for hours. It was hard work, but it gave me the opportunity to get to know many of these kids, and to listen and minister to them. After my son Joseph graduated from high school, my son John took over the leadership of the club, so my driving tasks continued for several years. There were many times when I felt overworked and under-appreciated. It was particularly disheartening when the club attendance was poor. But over the years the club produced an abundance of fruit by touching and changing the lives of hundreds of kids for God's glory. In addition, I enjoyed some recognition and reward when my involvement with the club enabled me to be on national radio with a congressman, as well as on local TV. I learned firsthand the truth behind 1 Peter

5:6 TLB, which says, "If you will humble yourselves under the mighty hand of God, in His good time He will lift you up."

I didn't know it at the time, but God was using my driving duties for the Bible club to prepare me for the ministry I have today. I learned a lot from listening to those kids pour their hearts out to me each week. I spent extra time in prayer and Bible study each day so that I could minister to them with the Word of God. It did my heart good to see what a difference it made in their lives. It still amazes me to think of how God used me to impact so many. I certainly didn't have much to offer anyone. I had spent the last two decades raising children and keeping a home. I think there's a lot of truth to that statement which says that "God doesn't choose those who are able, but those who are available." All I did was offer myself to the Lord for His purposes, and it wasn't long before He took me up on my offer. Romans 12:4-5 says, "There are different kinds of gifts, but the same Spirit. There are different kinds of service, but the same Lord." If you've accepted Christ as your Savior, you've been equipped to serve God and others for His glory. I guarantee that if you offer yourself and your God-given gifts to the Lord, He will show you how to put them to good use. Jesus said that He did not come to be served, but to serve, and He commands us to have the same attitude. (Matt. 20:25-28.) If the idea makes you fearful, I sympathize with you because I

LIVE ON PURPOSE TODAY

No matter how menial the task may seem at first thought, put your hand to something today in service to the Lord. Do it cheerfully and conscientiously. And then eagerly ask the Father, "What's next?"

have felt that way many times. God will help you overcome your fears if you ask Him, and He's promised to provide you with all the strength you need to perform your tasks. (1 Peter 4:11.) If you're already in active service, know that the Lord has promised you reward and promotion as you persevere and remain faithful. (1 Cor. 15:58; Matt. 25:23.) Remember that there are no "insignif-icant" jobs in God's kingdom. Every act of service we perform has great value in God's sight, even when we're not receiving thanks or recognition from others. Be encouraged by this precious promise from the Lord today: "God is not unjust; He will not forget your work and the love you have shown Him as you have helped His people and continue to help them"! (Heb. 6:10).

PRAYER

Lord, I thank You for equipping me to serve You and others. Today, I offer You all that I am and all that I have, and I ask that You use me for Your glory. Give me a spirit of humility, so that I'll be willing to "give myself to humble tasks" (Rom. 12:16 AMP). Help me to always serve enthusiastically. (Rom. 12:11 NLT.) Encourage my heart when my efforts are unnoticed and unappreciated. Thank You that as I'm faithful to serve, You are faithful to reward me!

God's Healing Word

My son, give attention to my words; incline your ear to my sayings. Do not let them depart from your sight; keep them in the midst of your heart. For they are LIFE *to those who find them, and* HEALTH *to all their whole body.*

PROVERBS 4:20-22 NASB

Years ago I sustained a severe shoulder injury in my aerobics exercise class. When the pain became intolerable, I saw my doctor, who prescribed some strong medication for me. For the next ten years absolutely nothing gave me relief from the relentless pain in my shoulder, and I began to resign myself to the fact that I would eventually have to undergo shoulder replacement surgery. When I wholeheartedly dedicated my life to the Lord and began studying His Word, I began developing a confidence in God's willingness to heal me. As I read through the Gospels, I couldn't help but notice that a major part of Jesus' ministry was devoted to healing people of their physical ailments. I began making lists of healing promises from the Bible, and I began praying and standing on them daily for my healing. It wasn't long before God led me to some supplements that were so effective for me that I've been completely pain free for almost eight years now.

If you find it hard to believe that Jesus is still in the business of healing today, you're not alone. A lot of believers share your view, and until eight years ago, I was one of them. While I admit that I still struggle with doubt sometimes, I can't deny the fact that since I began praying in faith for healing for myself and others, I have witnessed some incredible recoveries that have God's signature all over them. There's no question in my mind that the healing of my sore shoulder was a miracle. Medical tests showed that the damage to my joint was so severe that nothing short of major surgery would return it to normalcy. I certainly had prayed for healing during those ten years of agonizing pain, and I had others praying for me, too. But it wasn't until I began devoting myself to God and His Word that I received my healing. The Bible says that when we "attend" to God's Word (KJV), it is "life" to us and "health" to our whole body (Prov. 4:20-22). The original Hebrew word for "health" here can be translated as "medicine." I believe this means that when we give our attention to the Word of God—studying it, believing it, meditating on it, and doing what it says—it can benefit our bodies, as well as our spirits and souls. If I told my doctors that my severely injured shoulder was healed with supplements, they would never believe it. And neither do I. I believe that, just as God used a simple ointment of figs to heal King Hezekiah of a fatal illness after he prayed for healing (2 Kings 20:1-7), He used ordinary supplements to heal me of a damaged joint after I began praying and standing on His Word. The credit belongs to God, not to the remedy. I've discovered that when I pray for healing, it's wise for me

LIVE ON PURPOSE TODAY

Are you in need of healing? Do you suffer pain in your body? Take your medicine— take God's Word today! Begin reading God's healing promises, and when a particular verse is quickened to you, commit it to memory. Mediate on it day and night, and it will be health to your whole body.

not to do so with a specific remedy or pathway of healing in mind. Even if I've had the same ailment more than once, the Lord doesn't always lead me to the same solution each time. You'll recall that in the Gospels, Jesus often used various ways to heal people, even if they suffered from the exact same affliction. One reason for this may be that God doesn't want us putting our faith in a formula or a method, any more than He wants us putting our faith in a medicine or a doctor (as good and as necessary as they often are). He wants our faith to be in Him alone, and He wants us to seek Him first. I want you to know that I still have some health issues that I'm dealing with. But nowadays I don't just resign myself to living with health problems. I regularly seek God and persist in prayer for healing and wholeness, based on His promises. I don't lose heart as quickly as I used to, because the Bible says that it's through "faith *and* patience" that we inherit the promises of God (Heb. 6:12). Sometimes my prayers for healing are answered right away, and other times I've had to stand in faith for healing for weeks, months, or even years. But it's always been well worth the wait. If you are in need of healing today, don't despair. Put your faith in the Lord and attend to His Word, trusting that one day you'll be able to declare—"O Lord my God, I called to You for help and You healed me"! (Ps. 30:2).

PRAYER

Lord, teach me how to "attend" to Your Word, and how to pray Your perfect will concerning my health and healing needs. Remind me to give attention to the practical side of my health issues, as well as the spiritual. Show me when I should see a doctor, and give him Your wisdom and skill. Thank You for continually revealing Yourself to me as the Lord, my Healer! (Ex. 15:26.)

Anger Vs. Assistance

Everyone should be quick to listen, slow to speak and slow to become angry, for man's anger does not bring about the righteous life that God desires.

JAMES 1:19,20

Last week I lent my cellular phone to my son when he was going out. This wasn't exactly unusual, but what was unusual was the fact that after he returned home and I asked him to replace it in the recharger, he confessed that he didn't know where it was. We immediately began searching for it in every place we could imagine. As our search failed to uncover my phone, I felt that old familiar feeling of blood rushing to my head. My anger and frustration were building. I was tempted to say something to my son that I knew I'd have to repent for later. At the moment I figured it might be worth it. Just then God gave me a "knowing" that if I wanted His help, I needed to restrain my anger, pray, and leave the matter in His hands. As much as I wanted to vent my anger on my son, I wanted my phone back even more. So I told my son we would resume our search the following day and I went to bed, entrusting the matter to the Lord. The next day I told my husband about the missing phone. It only took him a minute or two to discover its location, and I knew it was God's way of teaching me about the importance of remaining calm and kind in the midst of turmoil.

The Bible says, "Keep your head in all situations" (2 Tim. 4:5). While it's the world's way to fly off the handle every time they feel like it, believers are gifted with Holy Spirit self-control (2 Tim. 1:7), and God expects us to make use of it in tense situations. At first glance it seems like worldly people have an unfair advantage because it's often easier to vent our anger, and it seems to make us feel better initially. But the truth is that the consequences these people suffer as a result of their unrestrained anger are ones that the Lord would rather spare us from. Ecclesiastes 7:9 says, "Do not be quickly provoked in your spirit, for anger resides in the lap of fools." And Proverbs 14:17 says, "A quick-tempered man does foolish things." Losing our cool will cause us to make mistakes in word and deed that we'll regret later on. It's just not worth it. Proverbs 15:18 NLT says, "A hothead starts fights; a cool-tempered person tries to stop them." Jesus has called us to be peacemakers (Matt. 5:9), and He has given us His Spirit so we have the ability and the desire to prevent and halt dissension, instead of contributing to it. One way we can do that is by saying the right thing at the right time. Proverbs 15:1 says, "A gentle answer turns away wrath, but a harsh word stirs up anger." Often we can deflect someone's anger by speaking words of gentleness and understanding. In cases like these, I've

LIVE ON PURPOSE

At your next opportunity to lose your temper, count to ten first—or even to twenty. And during that pause, allow the Holy Spirit to remind you of the importance of holding your tongue. Your reward will be God's help!

often whispered a silent prayer for help, claiming God's promise in Proverbs 16:1 AMP which says, "From the Lord comes the [wise] answer of the tongue." I used to think that I had to have the last word in situations like these if I wanted to come out on top. Now I know that it's often just the opposite. God has taught me that even if I appear to others to come out the loser, I will have won in His eyes, and He will reward me somehow. I think believers would be more motivated to resist anger if they knew how destructive it really is. Ephesians 4:26 NLT says, "Don't sin by letting anger gain control over you. Don't let the sun go down while you are still angry, for anger gives a mighty foothold to the devil." When we lose our temper, we may be opening the door for Satan to come in and "steal, kill and destroy" (John 10:10). That's why being patient is actually spiritual warfare. The next time you're in a tense situation, ask yourself which you want more— the "luxury" of venting your anger, or the rewards of God's help. I pray you'll choose the latter and discover for yourself that "a wonderful future lies before those who love peace" (Ps. 37:37 NLT).

PRAYER

Lord, show me how to cooperate with Your plan to develop more patience in me. Remind me that when I choose to lose my temper in a situation, I could be forfeiting Your help. When I do get angry, help me to "get over it quickly," as Your Word commands (Eph. 4:26 TLB). Thank You that by Your grace I'll be a peacemaker, instead of a troublemaker!

Let Your Light Shine

You are the light of the world. A city on a hill cannot be hidden.
Neither do people light a lamp and put it under a bowl. Instead
they put it on its stand, and it gives light to everyone in the
house. In the same way, let your light shine before men, that they
may see your good deeds and praise your Father in heaven.

MATTHEW 5:14-16

At a family gathering a few years ago, I couldn't help overhearing a discussion between my son John and a friend of the family. They were talking about a movie that was currently in the theaters and had a soundtrack of popular songs. When my son voiced his disapproval of the album because one of the song titles was an obscenity, I heard this friend exclaim, "Lighten up, John!" What was this friend saying to my son? She was basically saying, "C'mon, John, stop being so serious—and start thinking the way the rest of us do!"

Why do some folks—Christians and non-Christians alike—get so indignant when someone like John takes a stand against the popular culture? It makes them feel uncomfortable. It's like shining a spotlight on their questionable behavior for all the world to see. Jesus said that He wanted His followers to be salt and light to the world around them. (Matt. 5:13-16.) Why? Because it's the only way we can make a real difference for God on this earth. The apostle Paul wrote, "Have nothing to do with the fruitless deeds of darkness, but rather expose them" (Eph. 5:11). Naturally, we can use words to expose the sin around us, but there's an even better way. We can expose the works of darkness by our actions. There's an old saying that goes like this: "People may not believe what you say, but they'll believe what you *do!*" When mere words don't have an impact on the people around us, our Christlike behavior often can. In the same passage of Scripture, Paul goes on to say, "But when the light shines on them, it becomes clear how evil these things are. And where your light shines, it will expose their evil deeds" (Eph. 5:13,14 NLT). Every time that you and I "go along with the flow" of popular culture, our light for Christ dims and we lose an opportunity to draw others to Him. That's one reason why Paul continues with, "Be very careful then, how you live—not as unwise but as wise, making the most of every opportunity, because the days are evil" (Eph 5:15,16).

The following verse gets to the heart of the matter: "Therefore, do not be foolish, but understand what the Lord's will is" (Eph. 5:17). The only way we're going to be able to live a life that's pleasing to God, and one that will impact others for His kingdom, is to have a working knowledge of His Word. How did John know that the profane song title on that movie soundtrack was offensive to God? Because he was familiar with the Scripture that says, "But among you there must not be even a hint of sexual immorality, or of any kind of impurity, or of greed, because these are improper for God's holy people. Nor should

LIVE ON PURPOSE TODAY

All day long, be on the lookout for an opportunity to be a bold witness for Jesus Christ—a bold witness with a shining light. Allow your words and actions to uphold Bible standards even in a dark world.

there be obscenity, foolish talk or coarse joking, which are out of place, but rather thanksgiving" (Eph. 5:3,4). John didn't just have head knowledge of these verses, but he was applying them to his life and walking them out, instead of just talking about them. And people take notice. When John's at work and everyone around him is cursing and blaspheming, he refuses to join in. He doesn't hit people over the head with his Bible, but he lets his light shine through his words and actions. And he stands out in a crowd. Yes, there's a price to be paid when we live our lives for God. And there are untold sacrifices that we have to make daily. But the rewards far outweigh them all. Just ask John. Because of his faithfulness, the Lord is using him to touch the lives of millions of people each year for His glory. And if you were to ask my son, he'd tell you that he wouldn't want to live any other way. The next time you take a bold stand for the Lord and someone says to you, "Lighten up!"—don't forget that that's your cue to let your light shine!

PRAYER

Lord, give me the strength, the wisdom, and the courage I need to "go against the flow" of our worldly popular culture. Teach me how to devote myself to You and Your Word and to apply Your principles to my life so I can make a real difference for You. Thank You that as I take advantage of every opportunity that comes my way, You will use me to touch and change the lives of multitudes!

Not Perfect? Read This!

It is clear, then, that God's promise to give the whole earth to Abraham and his descendants was not because Abraham obeyed God's laws but because he trusted God to keep his promise. So if you still claim that God's blessings go to those who are "good enough," then you are saying that God's promises to those who have faith are meaningless, and faith is foolish. But the fact of the matter is this: when we try to gain God's blessing and salvation by keeping his laws we always end up under his anger, for we always fail to keep them. The only way we can keep from breaking laws is not to have any to break! So God's blessings are given to us by faith, as a free gift.

ROMANS 4:13-16 TLB

When I first saw these verses in the Bible, I underlined them and put stars all around them. Do you ever feel like you don't deserve God's gift of salvation? If you do, I know how you feel. These verses are for you as much as for me. They tell us that we don't have to earn salvation or God's love. We couldn't even if we wanted to. The truth is, we could never be "good enough" to save ourselves. That's exactly why God sent us a Savior. In fact, the Bible reveals that even our best efforts wouldn't measure up. Isaiah 64:6 says, "All our righteous acts are like filthy rags." But while we can't model perfection, we can model spiritual growth. Out of gratitude for God's gracious gift, we can seek to abide in Him and be fruitful for His glory. And we can serve Him and others out of a thankful heart.

In Ephesians 2:8-9, Paul writes, "For it is by grace you have been saved, through faith—and this not from yourselves, it is the gift of God—not by works, so that no one can boast." One reason why God wants to make our salvation a gift is so that we can't boast about it or take the credit for it. God wants the glory, and He deserves it. Scripture reveals that when people asked Jesus, "What must we do to do the works God requires?" He answered them, "The work of God is this: to believe in the one he has sent" (John 6:28,29). We all know how much Jesus spoke about the importance of our doing good works and loving and serving God, but here He gives us the bottom line. It's not what we do that matters most to God; it's in whom we believe. It's not what we do that makes us righteous in God's sight; it's what He has done for us. Does that mean that the Bible condones sin? Not at all. The same man who wrote the verses above in Romans 4, the apostle Paul, also wrote in Romans 6:2, "Shall we go on sinning so that grace may increase? By no means! We died to sin; how can we live in it any longer?" From the moment of salvation, we are empowered by the Holy Spirit to resist sin and obey God. We

LIVE ON PURPOSE TODAY

Spend a few moments today rejoicing in your free gift of salvation, serving God out of a thankful heart!

become increasingly uncomfortable with sin, and God's ways become more attractive to us. And Scripture assures us that "God is at work within us, helping us want to obey him, and then helping us do what he wants" (Phil. 2:13 TLB). I pray that these truths will help you to relax a little more and enjoy your special relationship with God. May you rest in this precious promise from

Him: "So now, since we have been made right in God's sight by faith in his promises, we can have real peace with him because of what Jesus Christ our Lord has done for us"! (Rom. 5:1 TLB).

PRAYER

Lord, forgive me for trying to earn the salvation You want me to receive as a free gift. Help me to stop striving to please You and to learn to abide and rest in You. Give me a revelation of my new identity in Christ so that I can cooperate with Your plan for my spiritual growth. Thank You for showing me that it's not my perfection that counts, but Yours!

Strength in Adversity

If you falter in times of trouble, how small is your strength!

PROVERBS 24:10

The Lord often shows me this verse when I'm going through difficult times. It's one of those "ouch" verses in the Bible, and it always convicts me when I see it. The Living Bible version says, "You are a poor specimen if you can't stand the pressure of adversity." God said basically the same thing to the prophet Jeremiah when he was complaining to the Lord about the injustices he had to deal with. "If you have raced with men on foot and they have worn you out, how can you compete with horses? If you stumble in safe country, how will you manage in the thickets by the Jordan?" (Jer. 12:5). In other words, "If you think this is bad, how are you going to handle it when things really get tough?" One reason why God wants us to be strong in times of trouble is because He wants to use us to advance the work of His kingdom. He can't do that if we fall apart every time we face a crisis in our lives. Can you imagine a commander putting weak and fearful soldiers on the front lines? Not only would his men get slaughtered, but he wouldn't have much chance of victory.

What does the Bible say about strength, and what can we do to appropriate the strength God wants us to demonstrate? Scripture says that the Lord Himself is our strength (Ps. 18:1), and we can declare Him as our strength, as David did. It says that the people who "know their God" (in a personal way) "shall be strong and carry out great exploits" (Dan. 11:32 NKJV). It also says that unconfessed sin can "sap our strength" (Ps. 32:4), so admitting our sin to God and receiving His forgiveness can restore us. The Bible tells us that "the joy of the Lord is our strength" (Neh. 8:10), so sadness and depression can make us weak. And we're told that we are strengthened when we trust in God and put our hope in Him. (Isa. 30:15; 40:31.) We can pray for strength, and we can stand on the many promises in God's Word concerning strength. In Psalm 86:16, David prayed, "Grant your strength to your servant." And in Psalm 18:32, David declared, "It is God who arms me with strength." The apostle Paul wrote, "I can do all things through Christ who strengthens me" (Phil. 4:13 NKJV), so we can be sure that God will give us the strength we need to handle all that He calls us to. Paul also writes, "Be strong in the Lord and in his mighty power" (Eph. 6:10), so we know that being strong involves our will and is something that we're capable of because of our relationship with God. And I have discovered that in times of crisis and weakness, praising God and giving Him thanks can build us up and strengthen us like nothing else can. May this promise from God encourage you today: "I command you—be strong and courageous! Do not be afraid or discouraged. For the Lord your God is with you wherever you go"! (Josh. 1:9 NLT).

LIVE ON PURPOSE TODAY

Thank and praise God today for His goodness and His mighty power. As the Lord becomes magnified in your eyes, adversity will become minimized, and renewed strength will be yours.

PRAYER

Lord, in times of trouble, show me how to stand strong so that I won't falter. Fill me with Your joy to give me strength, and help me to put my trust in You. Guard me from any unconfessed sin that could weaken me or hinder my fellowship with You. Let David's declaration be mine each day—"I love You, O Lord, my Strength!" (Ps. 18:1).

According to Your Faith

Then [Jesus] touched their eyes and said,
'According to your faith will it be done to you.'

MATTHEW 9:29

Maybe you've read the following imagined story of a scene in heaven. Some angels approach the throne and say, "Father, there is a mortal on earth asking for a blessing. What is Thy pleasure concerning his request?" The Father asks, "What did he send his faith in?" The angels answer, "He sent his faith in a thimble." The Father responds, "Well, fill the thimble with blessings and send it back to him. According to his faith, be it unto him." Again the angels come and say, "Father, another mortal is asking blessings of Thee." Again the Father inquires, "And what did he send his faith in?" The angels respond, "He sent his faith in a huge barrel." With a smile the Father says, "Fill the barrel with blessings and send it back to him. According to his faith, be it unto him."

Until I began seriously studying the Bible some years ago, I didn't know just how much of an impact my faith could have on my life and the lives of others. No one had ever told me that praying in faith, using my faith, and nurturing my faith were largely my responsibility. One of the verses that God used to begin opening my eyes to this truth is in Matthew 9:29 NKJV where Jesus says, "According to your faith let it be to you." The Savior spoke these words to two blind men who came to Him for healing, letting them know that the quality of their faith played a role in how the Lord responded to their request. The fact is that we *do* have a certain amount of control over our lives, and how we exercise our faith and trust in God *can* determine our outcome to some extent. While it's true that God *is* sovereign, He gives believers the awesome privilege of playing an important part in their own futures.

In addition, our faith and trust in God can make a tremendous difference in the lives of others. In Matthew 8:13, when Jesus said, "It will be done just as you believed it would," He was speaking to the centurion about the healing of his servant, not about the soldier's own healing, as in the case of the blind men. And in Mark 2:5 TLB, when four men brought their crippled friend to Jesus for healing, the Scripture says that the Savior healed the man "when Jesus saw how strongly they believed that He would help." I think it's interesting that the Bible doesn't reveal whether or not the ailing friend had faith for his own healing. It only talks about the faith of his friends, and apparently, that is what we're supposed to focus on. In Mark 9:20-24, when a distraught father comes to Jesus to ask for his son's healing, the Lord indicates that the man's faith will play a vital part in his son's fate. Jesus tells him, "Everything is possible for him who believes."

LIVE ON PURPOSE TODAY

Devote time to God's Word today—reading it, believing it, memorizing it, meditating on it, and obeying it. Your faith will grow by leaps and bounds!

We don't have to let these awesome truths intimidate us or make us fearful. Instead, we can thank God for making a way for us to make a major difference in our own lives and the lives of others. If it's your desire to have greater faith, ask the Lord to increase your faith daily. But don't stop there. Do your part by devoting yourself to God's Word—reading it, believing it, memorizing it, meditating on it, and obeying it. Before you know it, your faith will begin growing by leaps and bounds. And you'll begin experiencing more and more of the joy and satisfaction that come from bearing fruit for God's kingdom and glory. I heard a world-changing minister of the Gospel being interviewed one day. He was asked how he had accomplished so much for God. His answer was, "I always figured that if you've got a big God, you should ask Him for big things!" Don't play it safe with your faith. Start taking risks with it. The next time you have a need or seek a blessing from the Lord, don't send Him your faith in a thimble. Send it in a barrel overflowing with faith, knowing He'll return it to you overflowing with blessings!

PRAYER

Lord, it's my heart's desire to have great faith in You. I want not only to make a difference in my own life, but to touch and change the lives of others. Enable me to do that, Lord, and help me to do my part in the process. Thank You that my great and growing faith will bear an abundance of fruit for Your glory!

Grace Under Pressure

…Love your enemies, do good to those who hate you, bless those who curse you, pray for those who mistreat you…. Do to others as you would have them do to you…. If you love those who love you, what credit is that to you? Even 'sinners' love those who love them. And if you do good to those who are good to you, what credit is that to you? Even 'sinners' do that.

LUKE 6:27,28,31-33

Jesus makes it clear in these verses that He expects a lot from us, especially in the area of how we relate to others. Though it may be "natural" for us to respond to mistreatment with anger or hostility, we are called to live "supernatural" lives through the grace and power of the Holy Spirit living in us. Jesus is not impressed when we are good to those who are good to us, because even unbelievers are capable of doing that. But He expects us to do the right thing, even when the right thing is not being done to us. Jesus knew what it was like to be mistreated. He was kind, compassionate, and good, yet He was still persecuted wherever He went. And He warned His disciples that they could expect the same treatment. In John 15:18 and 20, Jesus tells us, "If the world hates you, keep in mind that it hated me first…. No servant is greater than his master. If they persecuted me, they will persecute you also." Knowing this, we have to decide if we are going to live our lives reacting like everyone else in these situations, or responding the way Jesus expects us to.

In chapter 12 of the Book of Romans, the apostle Paul teaches us how to respond to those who mistreat us. "Do not repay anyone evil for evil…. Do not take revenge, my friends, but leave room for God's wrath, for it is written: 'It is mine to avenge; I will repay,' says the Lord…. Do not be overcome by evil, but overcome evil with good" (vv. 17,19,21). It's God's job to judge others, not ours. If we take matters into our own hands, we don't "leave room for God's wrath," and God may not intervene in the situation at all because we haven't given Him place. He may feel that our retaliation is punishment enough for the one who wronged us. But if we leave the matter in God's hands, though we are letting the person off the hook, he is not off God's hook, and He will deal with them. When we release the wrongdoer to God, we are not excusing his actions; we are just forgiving him as an act of obedience to God. Don't expect your feelings to help you. You have to do it as an act of your will, and you may have to do it by faith. Often our feelings will fall in line after we do the right thing. Today, God is calling you to a higher level of faith, obedience, and reward. Let me encourage you with a promise from His Word: "Let us not get tired of doing what is right, for after a while we will reap a harvest of blessing if we don't get discouraged and give up"! (Gal. 6:9 TLB).

LIVE ON PURPOSE TODAY

If you discover even the slightest hostility in your heart toward anyone, forgive the person as an act of obedience to God. And be encouraged to know that even if you take this step *in* obedience and *by* faith, eventually your feelings will fall in line.

PRAYER

Lord, forgive me for the times I haven't acted Christlike when I've been treated unfairly. Help me to remember that You've placed a higher calling on my life and You expect much more from me. When I am mistreated, give me Your guidance and grace so that I may respond the way You want me to. Thank You that my witness will lead others to You!

The High Cost of Complaining

Do all things without grumbling or disputing; that you may prove yourselves to be blameless and innocent, children of God above reproach in the midst of a crooked and perverse generation, among whom you appear as lights in the world.

PHILIPPIANS 2:14,15 NASB

A few years ago I heard a well-known minister of the Gospel talking about some of the experiences he and his wife had during their early years of marriage. Even though he is enjoying abundant prosperity now, there was a time when all he and his family could afford was a cold water flat to live in. Times were hard, and he and his wife were tempted to complain about their hardships. But the Holy Spirit gave this godly man a "knowing" that if he wanted the Lord to bless him in extraordinary ways, he and his wife must never grumble about their circumstances. This man and his family were overwhelmed with joy when just a few years later they moved into a beautiful home with stately columns, surrounded by fragrant magnolia trees.

Before I began seriously studying the Bible, I didn't realize how destructive complaining could be. Now I know that it's offensive to God, and it can open the door for Satan to come into our lives to "steal, kill and destroy" (John 10:10). The Old Testament accounts of the Israelites wandering in the desert for 40 years reveal to us that God despised His people's complaints and often judged them for their grumbling. The apostle Paul refers to these accounts when he writes, "Don't grumble as some of them did, for that is why God sent his angel of death to destroy them. All these events happened to them as examples for us. They were written down to warn us..." (1 Cor. 10:10,11 NLT). The truth is that God takes our grumbling personally, and our complaints show a serious lack of gratitude for His boundless mercy and love for us. If you want to cut off the flow of God's blessings in your life, complaining is a good way to do it. On the other hand, being thankful for all He provides for us daily will cause Him to release His abundant blessings into our lives. How would you feel if you gave someone a gift and they responded with indifference, criticism, or complaint? How about if they were overjoyed and overflowing with thankfulness? Their response would naturally determine your treatment of them to a large degree. Should we be surprised if God feels the same way? It's all right to want to make progress and do better in various areas of our lives, but never to the extent that we fail to appreciate and give thanks for the blessings we already have. God expects more from His children than He does from the rest of the world. That's why He inspired Paul to write, "In everything you do, stay away from complaining and arguing, so that no one can speak a word of

LIVE ON PURPOSE TODAY

Pay close attention today to the words of your mouth. And if you hear yourself utter anything even close to a grumble, stop yourself in mid sentence. Replace every complaint with a word of praise from a thankful heart.

blame against you. You are to live clean, innocent lives as children of God in a dark world full of crooked and perverse people. Let your lives shine brightly before them" (Phil. 2:14,15 NLT). It's so natural for us to complain, that when we don't, we stand out—and people take notice. Do you really want to grab the attention of those people around you who desperately need the Lord in their lives? Refuse to complain or grumble when you're most tempted to. God promises that you'll make an impact on others when you obey Him in this area. The next time you've got the perfect opportunity to let loose with a few complaints, remember what it can cost you. Instead, let a grateful God reward you for resisting the urge to grumble!

PRAYER

Lord, forgive me for all the times I opened my mouth to grumble, instead of to give thanks. Give me a grateful heart, and teach me how to resist the urge to complain. When I obey You in this area, use my example to inspire others and draw them to You. Thank You for my present blessings, and for all those yet to come!

Prophesying Our Future

You will also declare a thing and it will be established for you.

JOB 22:28 NKJV

Some years ago, a relative of mine was involved in an incident that threatened to land him in prison. While we waited for the legal process to be accomplished, I went around telling people that if my loved one had to go to jail, I would have a nervous breakdown. I made the statement half-jokingly, but part of me really believed it. As it turned out, my relative *was* sentenced to prison, and within a year's time, my mental health broke down to the point where I needed tranquilizers, antidepressants, and psychiatric care just to cope.

The Lord brought this incident to my remembrance recently to highlight the impact my words can have on my own future. I was not a committed Christian at the time, and I had no working knowledge of the Bible. No one had ever told me that my words have authority in this earthly realm, and that the words I speak over myself can have awesome consequences. Proverbs 18:21 AMP says, "Death and life are in the power of the tongue, and they who indulge in it shall eat the fruit of it [for death or life]." I've heard some preaching that warns that we can literally prophesy our own futures to some extent. I've also learned that some well-respected ministers of the Gospel believe that Mark 11:23 can be taken in a negative sense, as well as a positive one. In this verse, Jesus says that whoever "believes that those things he says will come to pass, he will have whatever he says." What if it is true that this principle

LIFE ON PURPOSE DEVOTIONAL FOR WOMEN

can work in a negative sense? If so, then I shouldn't wonder why I actually did have mental health problems after voicing that I expected to have them. Job 22:28 NKJV says, "You will also declare a thing and it will be established for you." Verses like these have given me a holy fear concerning the words I speak over my life and the lives of others.

Sometimes I can't help wondering how I might have reacted to this same incident if it occurred after I became devoted to the Lord and His Word. I'd like to think that I might have had an attitude that said, "Yes, this will be hard to deal with at first, but God has promised to stick with me through the difficult times, and He will see me through it." I know now that when we and others speak negative things over our lives, they are not from God, but from our own fleshly attitudes or from Satan himself. And in these cases, Jeremiah 23:16 NKJV would apply: "They speak a vision of their own heart, not from the mouth of the Lord." I know this without a doubt because God says, "I know the plans I have for you; plans to prosper you and not to harm you, plans to give you hope and a future" (Jer. 29:11). When negative circumstances threaten to enter our lives, we don't have to expect to fall apart or to experience dark times. We don't have to anticipate being left without hope. We can cling to our God and

LIVE ON PURPOSE TODAY

Ask the Holy Spirit to help you guard your mouth and speak words of life. Begin to listen as you speak, and if you hear yourself speaking negative words—*stop!* Repent! And align the words of your mouth with God's Words that always produce abundant life.

His precious promises of supernatural assistance in our times of need. And we can confidently declare with the psalmist, "God is our refuge and strength, an ever-present help in trouble. Therefore, we will not fear, though the earth give way and the mountains fall into the heart of the sea..." (Ps. 46:1,2).

PRAYER

Lord, give me a keen awareness and a holy fear of how my words and attitudes can impact my future. Teach me how to speak words of life and hope over my own life and those of others. When troubles threaten to overwhelm me, remind me that with You by my side, I never need to expect to fall or fail. Thank You for planning a future filled with hope and good things for me!

In Times of Betrayal and Injustice

> *Then the king said to Zadok, "Take the ark of God*
> *back into the city. If I find favor in the Lord's eyes,*
> *he will bring me back and let me see it and his dwelling*
> *place again. But if he says, 'I am not pleased with you,'*
> *then let him do to me whatever seems good to him."*
>
> 2 SAMUEL 15:25,26

The above verses are from the Bible account of Absalom's plot to take the throne away from his father, King David. When Absalom leads a widespread revolt against his father, instead of David crushing the rebellion, he flees Jerusalem with those who have remained loyal to him. If you know anything about David, you know he was no coward. Many historians consider him the most courageous and successful warrior of all time. Yet here, he chooses to leave his beloved city behind so that it would be spared from certain destruction. While it takes great courage to stand and fight, sometimes it takes even greater courage to walk away and leave things in God's hands. These verses reveal the magnitude of David's faith in God. When faced with betrayal, injustice, and disappointment, he entrusts himself to the Lord and says basically, "Thy will be done."

Perhaps you've been in David's place at sometime in your life. If you've ever been passed over when you believed you deserved a promotion, you have an idea of how David must have felt. If the position at church or in school you thought you deserved went to someone else, you can empathize with him. If you've ever felt betrayed or unjustly mistreated by family members, you've been in David's shoes. David was a faithful servant of the Lord, and he loved God with all his heart. He made mistakes, and he suffered the conse-

LIVE ON PURPOSE TODAY

If you stick with God, you'll always come out on top. So, the next time unfairness and injustice rear their ugly heads, remind yourself that God is on your side. He will always take you to victory!

quences. He trusted God in the best of times and the worst of times. And even when his own son rebelled against him, David entrusted himself to the Lord, and God eventually restored him to his rightful place as king. First Peter 2:23 says that when Jesus was treated unjustly, "he entrusted himself to him who judges justly." Considering the outcome of their lives, do you think that David or the Master ever regretted leaving themselves in God's hands? No way. Next time you are confronted with injustice and disappointment, if you'll entrust yourself to the Lord, when all is said and done, He will honor you and lift you up!

PRAYER

Lord, I know that serving You doesn't guarantee that I'll always be treated fairly. But sometimes when I'm faced with unfairness, the hurt and bewilderment are just too much for me to bear. In times like these, remind me that Your Word says You are a "God of Justice." And give me the reassurance that You will work even my trials out for my good. Thank You that You are on my side!

From Trials to Triumphs

> *About midnight Paul and Silas were praying and singing hymns to God, and the other prisoners were listening to them. Suddenly there was such a violent earthquake that the foundations of the prison were shaken. At once all the prison doors flew open, and everybody's chains came loose.*
>
> ACTS 16:25,26

Paul and Silas were thrown into prison in Philippi for casting a demon out of a young slave girl who had been earning her master a lot of money. The disciples were stripped, beaten, and chained in a cell. The next thing that happened still amazes me, no matter how often I read it in Scripture. Paul and Silas began to pray and praise God in song. Most of us would have been grumbling and drowning in self-pity. We might have said something like, "God, here I am trying to serve You and lead others to You. How could You let these people do this to me? I don't deserve this!" Fortunately, instead of complaining, these disciples praised God, who responded by miraculously setting His servants free from captivity. As a result, the jailer and his entire household became believers.

Perhaps you are in a trial of your own today. Maybe the last thing you feel like doing is praising God. But listen to what Scripture teaches us. David said in Psalm 34:1, "I will bless the Lord at all times; his praise shall continually be in my mouth." And he meant it. Whether David was experiencing good times or bad, he praised God. Just one example of this is in 2 Samuel

12:20, where David and Bathsheba's infant son has just died as part of God's chastisement of the couple. The first thing David does is "go into the house of the Lord and worship God." This is just one of the many reasons why God called David a man after His own heart. And

LIVE ON PURPOSE TODAY

Whether you're experiencing an "up" or a "down"— and even if it's midnight in your circumstances—stop right now and offer up thanksgiving, praise, and worship to the Lord!

though the Lord allowed His servant to suffer the consequences of his sins, He gave David victory over all his enemies and blessed him with great wealth and honor. Paul and Silas praised God in the darkest of circumstances and unbelievers turned to Christ. If you'll praise God in your trials, your example could very well attract the attention of those who won't be reached any other way. Not only that, but you may find that the Lord will turn your trials into triumphs!

PRAYER

Lord, forgive me for the times I've grumbled and felt sorry for myself in times of trouble. I ask You to remind me that You deserve praise through all my ups and downs. Help me to realize how blessed I really am, and give me a thankful heart. Thank You that my example will change the lives of others for Your glory!

"Ungodly" Invitations

I never sat in the company of revelers, never made merry with them; I sat alone because your hand was on me and you had filled me with indignation.

JEREMIAH 15:17,18 NLT

In this passage, we learn how the great prophet Jeremiah had endured times of isolation and loneliness because of his devotion to the Lord. Those of us who have shunned invitations to participate in "questionable" social activities because of our commitment to God can really relate to Jeremiah's situation. Some of the things that many people consider harmless "fun" or "entertainment" can carry too high a price tag for the believer. Jesus said, "You are the salt of the earth. But if the salt loses its saltiness, how can it be made salty again? It is no longer good for anything, except to be thrown out and trampled by men" (Matt. 5:13). God has called us to be salt and light to the world. That means that He expects us to stand out, not blend in. The more we blend in with the rest of the world, the less of an impact we will have on it. In Jeremiah 15:19 NLT, God gave his devoted prophet this stern warning: "You are to influence them; do not let them influence you!" If God had to give someone like Jeremiah this admonition, how much more does it apply to us? In 1 Timothy 4:15-16, Paul writes, "Watch your life and your doctrine closely. Persevere in them, because if you do, you will save both yourself and your hearers." How badly do you want to be an effective witness to those around you? Do you have a burning desire to see others receive God's gift of salvation? Then you're going to have to make some serious personal sacrifices, even where your social life is concerned. You're going to have to be more discerning about your social activities, as well as the company you keep.

Our first obligation is to God, not to our friends or family. It's not uncommon for Satan to try to use even our closest loved ones to tempt us to go to places and do things that we know are not God's best for us. And since offering us invitations that don't interest us

LIVE ON PURPOSE TODAY

Pay special attention to the quality of Christian witness you convey today— and every day—and take stock in your activities. If necessary, begin saying, *"No!"*

aren't much of a temptation, the enemy's going to present us with opportunities that seem too good to turn down. "Ungodly" invitations can come in many forms. Movies, concerts, and parties are just a few examples. God wants us to be so sensitive to the leading of His Spirit that we will seek His wisdom and guidance when we make our social plans. Whenever you're confronted with an invitation that you don't have peace about, do not give your consent. Then let the Lord handle the consequences of your refusal. God promised Jeremiah that as a result of his devotion, He would make the prophet His spokesman. (Jer. 15:19.) Jeremiah was faithful, and God kept His promise. If you have a desire to be an instrument of God's power and grace, start saying "no" to some of the invitations that come your way. And know that when you do, you are opening the door for our great God to use you in awesome ways for His glory!

PRAYER

Lord, whenever I receive invitations of any kind, I ask that You remind me to seek Your approval before I accept. Don't let me forget that my first obligation is to You. Help me to be salt and light to this world so that I can influence others for good, instead of others influencing me in negative ways. Thank You that as I am faithful, You will use me to be a world-changer for Your glory!

A Prophet Without Honor

> Then Jesus told them, "A prophet is honored everywhere except in his own hometown and among his relatives and his own family."
>
> MARK 6:4 NLT

This verse has encouraged my heart many times when I've been hurt by the way my loved ones reacted to my commitment to God. The Bible reveals that some of Jesus' friends and family were not the least bit impressed with His ministry or His accomplishments. In fact, Scripture reveals that His own family thought He was "out of his mind" (Mark 3:21). Jesus was misunderstood because of His devotion to the Father and His dedication to the work His Father assigned Him. Why should we be surprised when our loved ones don't understand our commitment to God? The apostle Paul was often misunderstood, too. In 2 Corinthians 5:13 he says, "If we are out of our mind, it is for the sake of God." Seems to me that if people think we have lost our minds because of our love for God, we're in good company.

The truth is that when we decide to live for God, people are not always going to understand or respect us for it. Paul explains why: "The man without the Spirit does not accept the things that come from the Spirit of God, for they are foolishness to him, and he cannot understand them, because they are spiritually discerned" (1 Cor. 2:14). Now that we have the Holy Spirit living in us, we are able to see things from God's perspective. The way we view things will often be radically different than the way others do, and because of that, our priorities will be different. Have you ever accomplished something wonderful for God, and then been met with indifference and disinterest from your friends and loved ones? I have. It can turn our joy into hurt and frustration pretty quickly. Some time ago I gained some media attention because of my work for the Lord. Some of my friends and family were not the least bit impressed. What bothered me most was knowing that if I had been in the public eye because of a sports-related achievement, or because I

LIVE ON PURPOSE TODAY

These words of inspiration provide a timely opportunity to review the God-given dreams and goals you've outlined for yourself. If you've written down your goals, spend a few moments rereading them just now. If you haven't written them down before, do so now.
Live on purpose!

wrote romance novels, they would have been thrilled. But because I was being recognized for my service to God, they held no esteem for my accomplishments. That was a painful realization for me. Since then I've decided to serve the Lord with all my heart, even if no one else cares. Paul's words in Philippians 3:13-14 have been a great inspiration to me: "But one thing I do: forgetting what lies behind and reaching forward to what lies ahead, I press on toward the goal for the prize of the upward call of God in Christ Jesus." I'm going on with God. How about you?

PRAYER

Lord, thank You for the opportunities You've given me to serve You. Help me to remember that when others don't respect or honor my service to You, it doesn't diminish its value or usefulness in Your sight. Today I renew my wholehearted commitment to You, and I ask You to use me in new and exciting ways for Your glory!

Fulfilling Our
God-Given Purpose

{ *For we are God's workmanship, created in Christ Jesus to*
do good works, which God prepared in advance for us to do. }

EPHESIANS 2:10

Since my son John was a young teenager, he earnestly wanted to make a difference for God. The Lord led him to start a Christian Web site, Jesusfreakhideout.com, when he was only 16 years old, and it has steadily grown and reached more and more people each year. Even so, he has wrestled with feelings of discouragement and frustration from time to time. When he shares these feelings with me, I do my best to encourage him and to help him persevere. On one of these occasions recently, he was pouring out his heart to me and asking questions like—"How can I make a real difference when the grand scheme of things is so big? Is all of my seemingly endless work worth it? Does it have a point? Aren't there plenty of other people doing the same thing— and better? If they're getting more rewards than I am, does that mean I'm not on the right track? Sometimes I feel like I'm going against the wind—uphill!"

I not only sympathized with my son, but I empathized with him, too. I've often wrestled with many of these same feelings and questions, and I was painfully aware of what he was going through. After all, what am I doing for God that millions of other people aren't? Not only are countless people doing the same thing that I am, but many of them are doing it better, and achieving bigger and better results. Sometimes I feel like just one more little fish in a big sea of other little fish. On days when I let these things get me down, I try to remind myself of some uplifting truths that the Lord has taught me over the years. One of them is that I have been created by God with a very specific purpose in mind, and that He has prepared good works for me that only I can do. The Bible says, "For we are God's workmanship, created in Christ Jesus to do good works, which God prepared in advance for us to do" (Eph. 2:10). The Lord has prepared for me achievements that only I can accomplish in this life. Even the most gifted person in the world cannot accomplish my personal God-given assignments. It's entirely possible that there are lost people on this earth who will only be reached by me, as I carry out my God-given purpose and destiny. That fact alone is usually enough to keep me going when I'm tempted to quit and give up.

I've discovered that it's easy for me to lose my focus if I concentrate too much on what other people are doing. But if I stay focused on fulfilling the call of God on my own life, I can persevere in the toughest of times. I remind myself that God didn't create me to copy or imitate anyone else. He

LIVE ON PURPOSE TODAY

Articulate your God-given purpose in life to your spouse or close friend today. New vigor will rise up as you hear yourself share your own vision, and you'll be ready to run with it!

created me to fulfill my own unique God-given purpose and potential. And I can only do that by earnestly seeking His will for my life—by living each day in total dependence upon Him, and being sensitive and obedient to His Spirit's leading in all things. Scripture says, "The Lord will fulfill His purpose for me" (Ps. 138:8). As I concentrate on living for God and doing His will, I can count on Him to guide my steps in the paths that He has marked out for me. And I know that it's only in these paths that I will find the peace, joy, fulfillment, and success that are mine in Christ.

One thing's for sure—the devil does *not* want us to fulfill our God-given purpose and potential. He knows that if we do, we will wreak havoc on his kingdom of darkness, and we will be able to keep his interference in our lives to a minimum. He also knows that God will move heaven and earth to see that we receive all the good things He has in store for us. If it's your heart's desire to become all that God created you to be and to accomplish all the things He prepared for you in advance, please know that He will equip you with everything you need to succeed. I can't promise that you won't experience times of doubt or discouragement. But I *can* promise that if you'll keep your eyes on God and follow His lead, He will move mountains to make sure that His highest purposes for your life prevail!

PRAYER

Lord, today I offer You all that I am and all that I have.
I ask You to equip me with everything I need to fulfill my
God-given purpose and potential. Help me not to focus on
what others are doing, but to focus on You and Your call on
my life. Send me special encouragement when I get discouraged
or doubtful. Thank You that as I continually seek to follow
Your will for my life, I will enjoy divine favor, victory, and success!

He Lifts Us Up

The Lord lifts up those who are bowed down.

PSALM 146:8

I know what it's like to be "bowed down"—to feel beaten, depressed, weighed down, and defeated. If you've ever felt like that, this promise from God is for you, as much as it is for me. Sometimes our problems seem so overwhelming that we feel we're being crushed under the weight of them. Psalm 145:14 NLT says, "The Lord helps the fallen and lifts up those bent beneath their loads." It's never God's will for us to carry our own burdens, and His burden-bearing power is always available to us. But often we have to do our part in the process. The Bible tells us to cast our cares on the Lord. (Ps. 55:22; 1 Peter 5:7.) So we need to give our burdens to God in prayer, and then trust Him to sustain us according to His promise. James 4:10 NLT says, "When you bow down before the Lord and admit your dependence on Him, He will lift you up and give you honor." God is eager to rescue us, but many times He will wait for us to humble ourselves before Him and confess our need for Him. "I need You, Lord; please help me," is a simple but powerful prayer. In Psalm 3:3, David declares, "You are a shield around me, O Lord; you bestow glory on me and lift up my head." Many times, as in this verse and the previous one, "lifting up" is associated with our receiving glory and honor from the Lord, as well as comfort and deliverance. God isn't just interested in helping us live burden-free lives; He wants to help us live lives filled with success and victory!

Job 22:29 says, "When men are brought low and you say, 'Lift them up!' then He will save the downcast." God has promised that our prayers can make a difference in the lives of those who are discouraged and depressed. Likewise, when we are the ones in need of a

LIVE ON PURPOSE TODAY

Are you feeling bowed down? If so, pick up the phone and call that one the Lord prompts you to seek prayer support from. Don't delay and help will be on its way!

lift, it may be wise for us to seek out fellow believers who will intercede for us with the Lord. Ask God who you should request prayer support from, and then don't hesitate to receive the help He offers. When I go through difficult times that threaten to shake my faith, I remind myself of two things that I know without a doubt: (1) God is a good God, and (2) He loves us with a perfect love. This helps me to deal with the unanswered questions. We don't often think of an all-powerful God suffering along with us, but look at this verse in Isaiah 63:9 NLT: "In all their suffering He also suffered, and He personally rescued them. In His love and mercy He redeemed them. He lifted them up and carried them through all the years." I'm so thankful that we serve a God who feels our pain and desires only good for us. If you're in need of a lift today, let me encourage you to share your true feelings with the Lord. If your faith is faltering, be honest with Him and ask for His help. And have a good cry when you feel the need. God gave us tears for a reason, and they can be very healing. Stand on this promise from the Lord today: "You have allowed me to suffer much hardship, but you will restore me to life again and lift me up from the depths of the earth. You will restore me to even greater honor and comfort me once again"! (Ps. 71:20,21 NLT).

PRAYER

Lord, when I'm feeling bowed down, help me to turn to You in humility and honesty, and lift me up the way that only You can. Show me whom I should seek out for prayer support, and deliver me from the negative feelings that would hinder me from receiving their help. I don't just want to survive, Lord—I want to thrive! Thank You for lifting me up, and giving me honor and glory in Your name!

Dependence Vs. Independence

{ *Without Me, you can do nothing.* }

JOHN 15:5 NKJV

These words spoken by Jesus radically changed my life. I had grown up hearing that old saying, "God helps those who help themselves," so I believed that God wanted us to be independent and self-reliant. Then I discovered that, not only is this phrase not in the Bible, but it contradicts the principles of Scripture. Hebrews 11:6 TLB says, "You can never please God without faith, without depending on him." The truth is that God is pleased when we rely on Him and seek His help. Psalm 37:5 TLB says, "Commit everything you do to the Lord. Trust him to help you do it and he will." God wants to be partners with us in all our daily tasks and activities. When we invite God on the scene, an unlimited amount of resources and possibilities are made available to us. It's an "I can't, but God can" kind of lifestyle. And with God, there is no matter that concerns us which is too small or insignificant; there is no distinction between sacred and secular. God wants to be involved in every aspect of our lives, and He wants to help us reach our God-given potential. He also wants to ease our burdens and struggles. Psalm 34:5 NLT says, "Those who look to Him for help will be radiant with joy." Depending on God brings joy, peace, and satisfaction. But trying to accomplish things on our own makes us weary, frustrated, and discouraged. That's exactly why Satan wants us to think we don't need to ask God for help. He knows that the more we depend on God, the more productive and successful we'll be.

The apostle Paul said, "I can do all things through Christ who strengthens me" (Phil. 4:13 NKJV). Paul knew that his strength came from his dependence upon and union with Christ. Ours does, too. Asking God for help doesn't make us weak—it makes us strong. What really makes us weak is trying to do things on our own, in our own strength. Just try to be a parent, spouse, or student without God's help, and you will end up drained and defeated. But if you seek the Lord daily and depend on Him, He will sustain you and lead you to victory, no matter what challenges come your way. In 2 Corinthians 12:9 NLT, the Lord told Paul, "My power works best in your weakness." When we acknowledge our weaknesses and ask for God's help, it gives Him the opportunity to show what an awesome difference His involvement can make. It delights the heart of God when we say, "Lord, without You, I can do nothing. Please help me." Often I hear myself praying like this many times a day, especially when I'm tackling tough

LIVE ON PURPOSE TODAY

Prayerfully decide today which tasks you've been trying to handle on your own that could be handled much better with God's help. Hand them over to the Master!

situations and tasks. As a result, I've always discovered a newfound strength, peace, and confidence that enabled me to persevere and complete the task with joy. It's my prayer that you'll begin depending on God more each day so that you can join your praises with the psalmist who wrote, "Great is the Lord, who enjoys helping his servant"! (Ps. 60:12 NLT).

PRAYER

Lord, forgive me for failing to invite You to be a part of my daily endeavors. When I try to do things in my own strength, remind me to ask for Your help. Deliver me from an independent spirit, and enable me to depend on You more and more. Thank You for the peace, joy, and success that will be mine!

Saying "No" to Self-Pity

The bread of idleness (gossip, discontent, and self-pity)
she (the virtuous woman) will not eat.

PROVERBS 31:27 AMP

I recently went through some difficulties that got me so discouraged, that I found myself wrestling with feelings of self-pity. Years ago I might have played some sad songs and cried my eyes out, deriving a sort of perverse satisfaction from my misery. But this time I prayed and asked the Lord to help me resist these negative emotions. That's when He reminded me about some teaching I heard years ago about self-pity. I once heard a godly man say, "God is concerned about your hurt, but He doesn't want *you* concerned about it." This man went on to say that the reason self-pity is so destructive is that pride is at the root of it, and it causes us to focus too much on ourselves. I looked *self-pity* up in the dictionary and found the following definition: "Pity for oneself, especially pity that is self-indulgent or exaggerated."[3]

Psychiatrists have an interesting name for people who habitually indulge in self-pity—it's "injustice collector." These are the folks who are constantly dwelling on their hurts and hardships—whether real or imagined—and they enjoy thinking about them and talking about them. They lovingly collect and number each and every offense that others commit against them, and they search out people who will sympathize with them and commiserate with them. All this keeps the focus on themselves, which is what they want most. But this isn't God's way. He instructs us to walk in the God-kind of love, which is "not self-seeking," and which "keeps no record of wrongs" (1 Cor. 13:5). This is not to say that we should ignore or deny when we're being mistreated, but that we should take constructive action to see that we're treated with proper respect or to remove ourselves from harm's way, rather than sit idly by, feeling sorry for ourselves. Self-pity isn't just nonproductive—it's destructive. It can lead to bitterness, unforgiveness, and resentment. It doesn't bring people together—it divides them. And these are some of the reasons why Satan works so hard to get us to focus on our wounds rather than the cure—which is the love and wisdom of God. Throughout the pages of the Bible, God tells us again and again that He wants us to bring our hurts and sorrows to Him so that *He* can comfort us. He not only wants to be our Comforter, but our Vindicator. (Ps. 135:14.) If we'll let Him, He will defend us and fight our battles for us, leading us to victory every time. He tells us in His Word, "I, the Lord, love justice. I hate robbery and wrongdoing. I will faithfully reward my people for their suffering..." (Isa. 61:8 NLT).

A good antidote for self-pity is forgiveness. As we forgive those who offend us, we can let go of our negative emotions and ill-feelings toward

LIVE ON PURPOSE TODAY

Survey your heart and make sure that you're walking in forgiveness. That done, offer thanksgiving to the Father and enumerate the many blessings He has bestowed on you.

others, and we can receive the comfort and healing that can only come from God. Scripture says, "In all their suffering He also suffered, and He personally rescued them. In His love and mercy, He redeemed them. He lifted them up and carried them through all the years" (Isa. 63:9 NLT). God hurts when we hurt, and He wants to be our Deliverer. But we can block His efforts to comfort and rescue us when we insist on holding on to our feelings of resentment, bitterness, and unforgiveness. As we choose to forgive, we open the door to God's involvement, and all the blessings and provisions that entails. Another good antidote for self-pity is thankfulness. The Bible says, "Thank [God] in everything [no matter what the circumstances may be, be thankful and give thanks], for this is the will of God for you [who are] in Christ Jesus" (1 Thess. 5:18 AMP). No matter what is going on in our lives, we always have reason to give thanks to God and praise Him. Nothing is more offensive to God than our dwelling on our misfortunes and losses, and neglecting to recognize and enumerate all of the blessings He bestows on us daily.

Helen Keller said, "Self-pity is our worst enemy and if we yield to it, we can never do anything good in the world." We have been chosen by God, not just to live eternally with Him in heaven, but to make a difference for Him while we're still here on earth. Let's not allow self-pity to neutralize all the good we can do in this world in the name of Jesus.

PRAYER

Lord, please alert me whenever I begin to feel sorry for myself. Keep me from being overly-sensitive and self-absorbed, and teach me to bring all of my hurts and hardships straight to You. When I do, heal and comfort me the way that only You can. Give me the grace I need to forgive others quickly and thoroughly, and to praise You in all things. Thank You that as I resist self-pity in the power of Your Spirit, I will be rewarded by a gracious and grateful God!

An Invitation to Criticism

For I endure scorn for Your sake, and shame covers my face.
I am a stranger to my brothers, an alien to my own
mother's sons; for zeal for Your house consumes me,
and the insults of those who insult You fall on me.

PSALM 69:7-9

For me, these are some of the saddest verses in Scripture. The Bible says that God called David a man after His own heart. Yet many of the verses penned by this warrior-king reveal that he was often insulted and rejected because of his passion for God, even by his family and friends. Second Samuel 6 records that when David brought the ark of the covenant into Jerusalem, he "danced before the Lord with all his might," in celebration (v. 14). It says that when his wife, Michal, saw David's unrestrained enthusiasm for the Lord, she "despised him in her heart" (v. 16). When she criticized her husband for his public display of emotion, not only did David not apologize for it, but he informed her that he would become "even more undignified than this" in honor of the Lord (v. 22). The last verse in the chapter reveals that it is Michal, not David, who is judged by God, as she remains childless for the rest of her life.

In the Gospel of John, we see the same phrase, "zeal for Your house consumes me," attributed to Jesus when He rids the temple of moneychangers (John 2:17). When we display a Holy Spirit-inspired passion (or "zeal") for God, we are modeling the kind of devotion that the Son of God and David demonstrated. And just as they were often insulted and rejected, we will be, too.

LIVE ON PURPOSE TODAY

If you have suffered criticism, be encouraged and persevere today. Follow Jesus' own instructions and count yourself blessed if you've been put down. Focus on the applause you're receiving from heaven!

In Matthew 5:11-12 (MESSAGE) Jesus tells us how to react in those times: "Count yourselves blessed every time people put you down or throw you out or speak lies about you to discredit Me. What it means is that the truth is too close for comfort and they are uncomfortable. You can be glad when that happens—give a cheer, even!—for though they don't like it, I do! And all heaven applauds." We can take comfort in the fact that our devotion delights the heart of God. In Romans 12:11, Paul urges us to "Never be lacking in zeal, but keep your spiritual fervor, serving the Lord." Don't ever be ashamed because you serve God with enthusiasm. Isaiah 51:7-8 says, "Hear Me, you who know what is right, you people who have My law in your hearts: Do not fear the reproach of men or be terrified by their insults. For the moth will eat them up like a garment; the worm will devour them like wool." Our God is merciful, but He is also committed to His servants. Forgive and pray for the people who insult you, then let God deal with them. Rest in this promise from the Lord today: "Be happy if you are cursed and insulted for being a Christian, for when that happens the Spirit of God will come upon you with great glory"! (1 Peter 4:14 TLB).

PRAYER

Lord, teach me to serve You with a Spirit-led passion. When I'm criticized because of it, comfort me and help me to respond with a Christlike attitude. Guard me from feeling ashamed for displaying a holy zeal for You. May my devotion always invite applause from heaven!

Don't Get Offended

A man's wisdom gives him patience;
it is to his glory to overlook an offense.

PROVERBS 19:11

A re you easily offended? If you are, you have plenty of company these days. Our society has made becoming offended a national pastime. It's almost as if we've made offense a virtue today. One example of this is the prevalence of "road rage." One driver gets offended with another, and what began as a minor altercation can escalate into a major conflict. But that's not God's way. The verse above tells us that the honorable thing for us to do in these situations is to overlook the offense. If you want to defuse a volatile situation, refuse to become offended. Yes, you may have been wronged. And your feelings might have been hurt. But if you are a believer, God Himself has promised to be your Vindicator, and He will deal with those who treat you unfairly. (Ps. 135:14.) Your job is to handle situations like these His way, not the world's way. Psalm 119:165 AMP says, "Great peace have they who love Your law; nothing shall offend them or make them stumble." If we are lovers and doers of God's Word, we will walk in peace and we will not be easily offended. When the apostle Paul is describing the God-kind of love that believers are to demonstrate, he says, "It is not rude, it is not self-seeking, it is not easily angered, it keeps no record of wrongs" (1 Cor. 13:5). The next time you are tempted to take offense at something someone says to you, pray and ask the Lord, "Is there any truth to this, Lord? Do I need to make some changes here?" Then be honest with yourself and God, and let Him deal with you, if necessary.

Proverbs 18:19 says, "An offended brother is more unyielding than a fortified city." Is there someone in your life, like a family

LIVE ON PURPOSE TODAY

Determine to see just how many doors you can slam in the devil's face today by forgiving every offense that comes your way!

member, who gets offended easily, and whom you have to deal with on a regular basis? People like these can be difficult to get along with because when they take offense, they refuse to listen to reason or to yield to attempts to make amends. We may not always be able to avoid offending these people, but there are a couple of things we can do. We can pray for them, and we can refuse to become offended ourselves. The reason taking offense is displeasing to God is that it's destructive to relationships. It divides people and causes conflict. It can break up families, friendships, and even churches. It's one of Satan's most valuable weapons against God's kingdom, and as believers, we are to be aware of his tactics so that we won't become his victims. (2 Cor. 2:11.) Proverbs 17:9 AMP says, "He who covers and forgives an offense seeks love, but he who repeats or harps on a matter separates even close friends." Every time we forgive an offense, we are preserving our relationships and slamming the door in the devil's face. Most of all, we are pleasing and glorifying the One who deserves our very best!

PRAYER

Lord, You know better than anyone how many opportunities to take offense I encounter each day. I ask that You give me the grace I need to resist becoming offended in these situations. Make me an example and an inspiration to others. Deal with me when I'm in the wrong and I need to make some changes. When I suffer hurt, heal and comfort me. Thank You that by Your grace, I shall walk in peace!

The Power of God's Word

The Word of God is full of living power.
It is sharper than the sharpest knife, cutting
deep into our innermost thoughts and desires.

HEBREWS 4:12 NLT

I once read a true story about how a minister spoke God's Word over a friend in the hospital and witnessed its powerful effect on the patient's heart monitor, as well as on the patient herself. Here was modern technology recording and confirming the inherent power in God's Holy Word.

I'm convinced that if believers had a real awareness of just how powerful God's Word is, they would pay more attention to it. When Joshua was taking over Moses' job, God told him to meditate on His Word day and night. The Lord told Joshua that this was how he would be able to perform the will of God and be prosperous and successful. (Josh. 1:8.) And in Proverbs 4:20-22, the Lord says that His Word is life and health to those who pay attention to it. If you're willing to invest some time and energy reading, memorizing, and meditating on the Word of God, you can experience dramatic, positive changes in every area of your life. Let me share with you some simple but powerful principles that the Lord has shown me in recent years.

We can honor God by quoting and meditating on His Word three ways: (1) by putting a verse in prayer form, (2) by making it a declaration of faith, and (3) by turning it into an expression of praise. For example, each day I pray, "Lord, order my steps this day," which is based on Psalm 37:23 KJV. Then throughout the day I reaffirm God's answer to my prayer for guidance by declaring, "My steps are ordered by the Lord!" If doubt and fear begin to assail me, I encourage myself by praising Him for the answer with, "Thank You, Lord, that my steps are ordered by You!" If I have a need, I claim Philippians 4:19 and quote it according to my specific need. "Thank You, Lord, that You supply all my job needs!" I have used this verse to seek God for every conceivable need, including financial, healing, material, and social needs. I combine my faith with my declarations, according to Hebrews 4:2, and as a result, rest and peace flood my mind and heart. God's Word has the ability to build our faith, renew our minds, and change our hearts. If we don't meditate on God's truths day and night, we will be easy targets for Satan's deceptions. Declaring God's Word is not mind over matter—it's truth over error. Jesus used Scripture to defeat Satan when he came to tempt the Savior in the wilderness, and we can do the same thing. (Luke 4:1-12.) Each day of our lives, we have two choices—we can meditate on God's promises, or we can meditate on our problems. Meditating on God's Word can bring peace, joy, life, and health.

LIVE ON PURPOSE TODAY

Declare God's Word as truth over error in your life today and honor God by quoting and meditating on His Word in the three ways shared: Put a verse in prayer form, make it a declaration of faith, and turn it into an expression of praise.

Meditating on our problems can cause anxiety, fear, despair, and sickness. The Bible tells us to "be imitators of God" (Eph. 5:1). Do you think God is wringing His hands, wondering what He's going to do about our problems? No way. The Bible says He's "watching over His Word to perform and fulfill it" on our behalf (Jer. 1:12). So let's give Him something to work with. Let's honor our God by letting Him hear His precious Word on our lips day and night, for only then will we be prosperous and successful for His glory!

PRAYER

Lord, fill my heart with a growing passion for Your Word.
Help me to believe, declare, and act upon it for my good and
Your glory. Show me how to apply Your truth to every area
of my life. Thank You, Lord, that Your Word is true and
You are true to Your Word! (John 17:17; Heb. 11:11 AMP.)

Even Now

But I know that even now God will give you whatever you ask.

JOHN 11:22

These words were spoken to Jesus by Martha, the sister of Lazarus. Her brother had already been dead four days by the time Jesus arrived. Yet here she confesses her faith in the Savior to do even the impossible. Moments later Martha witnesses a miracle as her brother is raised to life by the Master.

A few years ago God began bringing me up to a new level of faith. He taught me how to pray what I now refer to as my "even now" prayers. I would be facing an impossible situation, and it would seem like all the doors before me had been closed. My first impression would be to think, *I guess it just wasn't God's will.* Then I would sense another impression coming up in my spirit telling me to continue praying in faith. I might pray something like this: "Lord, I admit this looks like a hopeless situation, but I know that even now, You can make a way where there seems to be none. I ask that You do that, Lord." I have seen so many seemingly closed doors opened by praying like this, that my prayer life has been radically changed forever. And I have used this principle in praying about small matters, as well as big ones.

Jesus said, "The things which are impossible with men are possible with God" (Luke 18:27 NKJV). I think it's sad that our society has gotten so sophisticated and cynical that we've forgotten how to pray for the impossible. In Jeremiah 32:27, the Lord says, "I am the Lord, the God of all mankind. Is anything too hard for me?" This statement should not only encourage us, but it should convict us as well. Psalm 77:19 TLB says, "Your road led by a pathway through the sea—a pathway no one knew was there!" The Israelites never could have imagined that God would make a way for them through the Red Sea. Likewise, when we pray for the impossible, God will often make a way for us that will exceed our expectations. Psalm 77:14

LIVE ON PURPOSE TODAY

Can you think of a dream or vision that you have given up on because it looked like it would never come to pass? Are there seemingly impossible situations in your life where you gave up too soon? If so, call upon the Holy Spirit to lead you into an "even now" prayer!

TLB says, "You are the God of miracles and wonders! You still demonstrate your awesome power." When we ask God for the impossible, we invite Him to work wonders in our lives—something He delights in doing. Have you given up on a dream or vision that God has planted in your heart, because at this point it looks like it can never come to pass? What "impossible" situations do you have in your life right now that maybe you've given up on too soon? Perhaps the Lord is just waiting for you to come to Him in faith today, saying, "Lord, I know that even now...."

PRAYER

Lord, I ask that You increase my faith and expand my vision so that I can trust You to do the impossible in my life. Help me to never put limits on You. When I'm tempted to give up on a situation too soon, remind me to ask You to make a way where there seems to be none. Thank You that You are the God of the impossible!

Don't Get Lazy

Don't drag your feet. Be like those who stay the course with committed faith and then get everything promised to them.

HEBREWS 6:12 MESSAGE

Recently, some of the problems my family and I had experienced in our neighborhood in the past arose once again. When they first resurfaced, I felt somewhat confused and bewildered. I had prayed and stood on God's promises for peace for my "borders" (Ps. 147:14), and I had witnessed the delivering power of God in mighty ways. But I had begun to take God's blessings for granted. When the problems threatened once again, I sought the Lord for the reason. He promptly pointed out to me that my prayers in that area had gone from earnest to anemic. And He reminded me that I needed to continue to stand in faith for the peace of my neighborhood if I wanted to regain and maintain the victory I had won before.

Hebrews 6:12 says, "We do not want you to become lazy, but to imitate those who through faith and patience inherit what has been promised." I realized that I had become a "spiritual sluggard"—as the Amplified Bible version of this verse says—at least where this issue was concerned. When the problem was at its worst, I used my faith and patience to lay hold of God's promises for the situation. But as soon as the problem showed signs of subsiding, I slacked off. That was a big mistake. Even so, it was a reminder of how important it is for us to continue to stand in faith for God's blessings, even when it looks like our prayers have

already been answered.
Proverbs 13:4 says, "The
sluggard craves and gets
nothing, but the desires
of the diligent are fully
satisfied." Those of us
who want God's blessings
badly enough to diligently
pray for them will find
that diligence produces
results. Do you ever feel
like you want to take a

LIVE ON PURPOSE TODAY

Don't make the devil's job
easy today! Instead, ask
yourself if there are areas in
your life in which you've
spiritually "slacked off"!
Armed with that information,
stand on the promises of God
and pray with new vigor.

"spiritual vacation"? I do. There are days when I wake up and
think, *I don't feel like praying or standing on God's promises today. I don't
feel like reading my Bible or seeking God's face.* But I have found that
spiritual passivity can be very costly. Are there areas in your life in
which you've spiritually "slacked off"? If so, you may be hindering
the flow of God's blessings into your life. Don't make the devil's
job easy for him. Satan is relentless, and we need to be relentless,
too. Talk to the Lord about any areas in your life that you might
be neglecting spiritually. And ask Him to help you get back on
track. It won't be long before you're reaping a harvest of blessings
that keeps on coming!

PRAYER

*Lord, forgive me for the times that I've been a "spiritual sluggard."
Give me the grace I need to stand in faith for all of the blessings You
have in store for me and my loved ones. When I'm tempted to take a
"spiritual vacation," remind me of what it can cost me. Thank You
that my diligence will defeat the enemy and glorify You!*

Endnotes

[1] *Webster's New World Thesaurus*, 3d. ed. (New York: Macmillan, 1997 Simon & Schuster), s.v. "strife."

[2] *Webster's New World™, College Dictionary*, 3d. ed. (New York: Macmillan, 1996 Simon & Schuster), s.v. "sustain."

[3] *Webster's New World™, College Dictionary*, 3d. ed., (New York: Macmillan, 1996 Simon & Schuster), s.v. "self-pity."

Prayer of Salvation

God loves you—no matter who you are, no matter what your past. God loves you so much that He gave His one and only begotten Son for you. The Bible tells us that "...whoever believes in him shall not perish but have eternal life" (John 3:16). Jesus laid down His life and rose again so that we could spend eternity with Him in heaven and experience His absolute best on earth. If you would like to receive Jesus into your life, say the following prayer out loud and mean it from your heart.

Heavenly Father, I come to You admitting that I am a sinner. Right now, I choose to turn away from sin, and I ask You to cleanse me of all unrighteousness. I believe that Your Son, Jesus, died on the cross to take away my sins. I also believe that He rose again from the dead so that I might be forgiven of my sins and made righteous through faith in Him. I call upon the name of Jesus Christ to be the Savior and Lord of my life. Jesus, I choose to follow You and ask that You fill me with the power of the Holy Spirit. I declare that right now I am a child of God. I am free from sin and full of the righteousness of God. I am saved in Jesus' name. Amen.

If you prayed this prayer to receive Jesus Christ as your Savior for the first time, please contact us on the Web at **www.harrisonhouse.com** to receive a free book.

Or you may write to us at
Harrison House
P.O. Box 35035
Tulsa, Oklahoma 74153

About the Author

J. M. Farro, gifted writer and author, reaches out to thousands of people through **www.jesus freakhideout.com**. Since 1996, this popular web site has grown in scope and outreach beyond the boundaries of the Christian music  industry. Their focus is album reviews, artist information, interviews, music news, and ministry through devotionals and prayer. On staff since 1998, J. M. Farro counsels thousands of men and women around the globe each year through her devotionals and prayer ministry. She and her husband, Joe, have two sons. They make their home in Nazareth, Pennsylvania.

To contact J.M. Farro, please write to:

J. M. Farro
P.O. Box 434
Nazareth, PA 18064

Or you may email her at:
farro@jesusfreakhideout.com
or jmf@jmfarro.com

Please include your prayer requests and comments when you write.

Other Books by J.M. Farro

Life on Purpose™ Devotional for Men
Life on Purpose™ Devotional

www.harrisonhouse.com

Fast. Easy. Convenient!

- ◆ New Book Information
- ◆ Look Inside the Book
- ◆ Press Releases
- ◆ Bestsellers

- ◆ Free E-News
- ◆ Author Biographies
- ◆ Upcoming Books
- ◆ Share Your Testimony

For the latest in book news and author information, please visit us on the Web at www.harrisonhouse.com. Get up-to-date pictures and details on all our powerful and life-changing products. Sign up for our e-mail newsletter, *Friends of the House,* and receive free monthly information on our authors and products including testimonials, author announcements, and more!

Harrison House—
Books That Bring Hope, Books That Bring Change

The Harrison House Vision

Proclaiming the truth and the power

Of the Gospel of Jesus Christ

With excellence;

Challenging Christians to

Live victoriously,

Grow spiritually,

Know God intimately.